THANK YOU
FOR COMING
TO HATTIESBURG

THANK YOU FOR COMING TO HATTIESBURG

ONE COMEDIAN'S TOUR OF NOT-QUITE-THE-BIGGEST CITIES IN THE WORLD

Todd Barry

GALLERY BOOKS

NEW YORK   LONDON   TORONTO   SYDNEY   NEW DELHI

G

Gallery Books
An Imprint of Simon & Schuster, Inc.
1230 Avenue of the Americas
New York, NY 10020

Copyright © 2017 by Todd Barry

All photos courtesy of the author.

First Gallery Books hardcover edition March 2017

GALLERY BOOKS and colophon are registered trademarks of Simon & Schuster, Inc.

For information about special discounts for bulk purchases, please contact Simon & Schuster Special Sales at 1-866-506-1949 or business@simonandschuster.com.

The Simon & Schuster Speakers Bureau can bring authors to your live event. For more information or to book an event contact the Simon & Schuster Speakers Bureau at 1-866-248-3049 or visit our website at www.simonspeakers.com.

Manufactured in the United States of America

10   9   8   7   6   5   4   3   2   1

Library of Congress Cataloging-in-Publication Data is available.

ISBN 978-1-5011-1742-8
ISBN 978-1-5011-1744-2 (ebook)

CONTENTS

FOREWORD

JESSE EISENBERG

It's always a crapshoot when two things you love join forces.

Sometimes it's a perfect union. For example, I love Stephen Sondheim and I love history. So when I discovered Stephen Sondheim's musical about the opening of Japan's borders in 1853 (*Pacific Overtures*), I felt it had been written exclusively for me.

Or when my friend Lee got a treadmill in his apartment. I love running on treadmills and I love hanging out with Lee. Another perfect union at the center of my personal Venn diagram.

But sometimes, this marriage doesn't work out so well: For the last several years, I loved watching the scrappy Golden State Warriors basketball team. During this time, I also loved watching the elegant Kevin Durant, who played for the Oklahoma City Thunder. But this summer, Kevin Durant joined the Golden State Warriors and they became that horrible, elitist Goliath that so often ruins competitive sports. They became too much of something good; the double-stuffed Oreo, the *ménage à trois,* the thirty-minute shower.

So when Todd Barry told me that he was writing an anthropological travelogue of the secondary cities on the standup comedy touring circuit, I was cautiously excited.

I love reading travelogues (Pico Iyer, Paul Theroux, Rory Stewart) and my degree in college is anthropology. I'm from New York City but currently living in a secondary Midwestern city and I love analyzing the differences and immersing myself in what feels different.

I also love standup comedy. In particular, I love Todd Barry's standup comedy. I have listened to Todd's albums so many times that, at one point, they were my go-to comforting sounds in moments of distress. That is, Todd Barry's wry observations about modern life were my Babbling Brook, my Autumn Thunderstorm.

Luckily, I discovered that Todd's hysterical travelogue, *Thank You for Coming to Hattiesburg*, delivers on my high—and very specific—expectations; it is *Pacific Overtures*, it is Lee's treadmill. It is not Kevin Durant's Warriors.

But what makes these stories really compelling is that, just like in his standup, Todd manages to create a self-portrait that is as honest as it is enigmatic. In his standup, Todd masterfully performs as a kind of neurotic braggart, somehow convincing as a man who a) lives in a ten-room apartment and b) recently bought his parents a crack house because he couldn't afford to buy them an upgraded suburban home. In his standup, he dates Julia Roberts but is too nervous to talk to strangers; he's as successful as the Rolling Stones, but still receives e-mails from the audience asking what time his shows will begin. Is it hubris? Is it self-deprecation? It's not really either and it's not really both.

Todd is an enigma. And this book, by design, does little to unravel him. But if you choose to wade through his funny anecdotes and ironic reflections, you will begin to see the portrait of a performer who, like any great performer, worries about their craft. Like all thoughtful artists, Todd is much more likely to remember his one bad South Bend, Indiana, show than the ninety-nine shows that went perfectly. To paraphrase a telling line of his, "The show must have gone well because I don't remember it." He fastidiously assesses how many people were at each venue, analyzes the effect that the height of the stage and the opening act have on his performance (an analysis I found most surprising), and laments the location of most venues' bathrooms, which force him to be seen by the audience prior to a show. Whether intentional or not, Todd reveals himself to be someone who is obsessively vigilant about his work and he is able to thoughtfully (and humorously) contextualize it for us.

And that's what makes *Thank You for Coming to Hattiesburg* such a successful travelogue. Its nominal focus is on secondary cities on the standup comedy circuit, but it ends up revealing the experiences of someone who cares deeply about what they do.

FOREWORD

DOUG STANHOPE

I read Todd Barry's *Thank You for Coming to Hattiesburg* in the intensive care unit of Tucson's University Medical Center while waiting for my wife to come out of a coma. Of course I hadn't seen the coma thing coming when I'd initially agreed to write the foreword for Todd's book and was surprised when Todd said not to even worry about writing it under the grave circumstances. I kind of expected him to say something to the effect of "But you did promise . . ."

I underestimated his humanity.

Also, I had already had to cancel my own tour due to this disastrous turn of events, some gigs specifically mentioned in Todd's book. I've prided myself that in more than twenty-five years in comedy, I've never canceled a show for any personal reason save for a few rare television appearances. I knew that reading his book would reinforce why my wife's life might be more important than disappointing a boozed herd of humps at Sally Tomatoes in Rohnert Park, California.

Todd and I both have an affinity for playing "secondary markets" as he likes to call them. I refer to them as "shitholes" generally. We enjoy them for a lot of the same reasons. The appreciation of small-town audiences, the lack of stress, the curiosity of visiting new places.

But while Todd and I cover quite a bit of the same territory, a lot of the same small comedy clubs or stinking roadhouses, we almost never cross paths. Todd is a different kind of animal. While you will find him in your finer coffeehouse, I will be slumped over the mahogany of your most barren gin joint. Todd will be complaining about the grimy condition of the club's toilet, unaware that I was the one who befouled it so egregiously in the weeks prior. Todd wants bottled water in his greenroom. I'm happy to even have a greenroom, and the only time I drink a bottled water is if I need to empty it in order to have something to piss in when the greenroom has no toilet. And then I'm upset I had to drink water.

Todd Barry's book will no doubt give you plenty of insight into the life of a comedian on the road in Middle America. You'll learn our distinct nomenclature, do's and don'ts and how to not be an aggravation as either a new comedian or an overzealous audience member. Even I was perplexed at some comedy bombs he dropped within these pages. He speaks of things like "contracts" and "riders," ideas foreign to me when shoveling out a load of drunken vitriol and sodomy jokes in Little Rock. I'm usually drunk enough by the time I get paid that I simply have to put blind trust in the paymaster, like a blind man counting on human decency that the currency he's been handed is in the proper denominations.

Todd uses spreadsheets, apps, and programs to keep track and organize his payments and expenses. I have balls of receipts in my pockets, some with poorly scribbled notes on the back, some that have been through the laundry. He gets uneasy when he spots an audience member who's too intoxicated. I freak out if I spot one more sober than me.

Yet we are both still drawn to these much neglected gems of the road less trampled. Brand-name comedy club chains serve their purpose, but if you limit yourself to only the safe bets, you'll never see anything new or frightening or fun. You need to jump into the muck if you wanna wake up with a good story. The more hideous the better for me. I love to complain about the shitholes because that's where the funny lives along with the bacteria. Todd loves to complain too but I think it's because he really likes to complain and really doesn't like fungus. To each his own.

And speaking of bacteria, I'll close with an update on the old lady. During this read she did in fact wake from her coma after nearly a week. I assume Todd will take full credit and expect an invoice. But shortly afterward my wife developed the superbug known as C. diff. This means all visitors must wear smocks and rubber gloves and that anything that is to be removed from this room where I write (in rubber gloves) must be completely sterilized or thrown in the trash. As it would be impossible to Purell every page of Todd's book—much less smearing all the pages—I had to complete my reading of it inside her room and now it will be incinerated with the sheets et al.

And I'm sure he will use this quote: "Todd Barry's *Hattiesburg* book is comedy at its most toxic!" or perhaps "It's the comedy equivalent of *Fahrenheit 451!*" or simply "Burn This Book!"

Finally, Todd has a way of pretending to demean himself in this book with his referring to his brilliantly crafted jokes and the like, as though he is being sarcastic. He isn't. He and any comedian who has ever watched him knows that he is one of the mostly truly gifted and skilled wordsmiths and creators in the world of comedy. Even when that world takes a detour to the other side of the tracks. Probably in some shithole down the street from you.

At Madison Square Garden before the tour.

INTRODUCTION

Hello. It's Todd Barry. Yes, the massively famous comedian. You may have seen me do standup on *The Late Show with David Letterman*, *Conan*, or Comedy Central, or some of my *spot-on* acting in the TV shows *Louie, Flight of the Conchords*, and *The Larry Sanders Show*, or in the movies *The Wrestler* and *Road Trip*. I could go on and on listing my credits, but I don't want this intro to be longer than that very long book *War and Peace*! Actually let's do one more. I had a comedy special/documentary called *The Crowd Work Tour*, where I did a whole tour without any material. I just bantered with the audience. It might still be on Netflix when you read this.

I made my standup comedy debut at the open mic night at Coconuts Comedy Club, located in a Howard Johnson's hotel in North Miami Beach, Florida, on May 1, 1987. It was right at the height of the famous *comedy boom* of the eighties, where there was a proliferation of comedy clubs, and every bar that had a stage or a floor (or at the sports bar I played in Massachusetts, a boxing ring) would have a comedy night. There was comedy everywhere, and if the club had an open mic night, you could decide to be a comedian on Sunday and be onstage on Monday. Back then, a lot of comedy clubs made their open mic night part of the regular headliner's show, so you would play to a real audience, then the audience would watch a couple of touring pros. Nowadays, especially in cities like New York or Los Angeles, the open mic nights are at bars, and comics often perform for other comics who are waiting to go on.

I've never been a *road dog*—some guys are out there forty weeks a year—but I do my share of touring. It pays my rent, and I think it's important to bring the comedy to the people. Sometimes I play big cities. Other times not-so-big cities. These are known as *secondary markets*. Sometimes they're even known as *tertiary markets*, although it's unlikely you'll hear a comic say, "I'm gonna tear up some *tertiary markets* this summer. Those *tertiary markets* don't know what's about to hit them!"

In 2011 I was about to go on tour with two comic pals, Neil Hamburger (real name Gregg Turkington) and Brendon Walsh. The plan was to do eight shows in nine days. At the last minute our agent called: "Would you guys want to do a show in Toledo on the day off?"

Hmmm. Toledo? Instead of a day off? Um, no? I don't think so? Do I? "Gregg, what do you think?" He said he'd go either way, so it was up to me. I'm not always great with decisions. I liked the idea of a day off, but to quote Mike Watt, bass player for punk band Minutemen, "If you're not playing, you're paying." We wouldn't make money that off night and would still have to get hotel rooms. Those were practical concerns, but there was something else to consider: I'd never been to Toledo. *When will I ever get a chance to go to Toledo? Yeah, let's do it! We're going to Toledo!*

I don't remember how the show went there, but I don't remember it being bad, so that means it was good. And we did have one particular moment preshow that I quite enjoyed. When we got to the venue we were ushered into a shabby "dressing room" (or *greenroom*; I still don't know the difference. I'll use these interchangeably throughout the book) that also doubled as a storage room. Actually, it was a storage room that doubled as a dressing room. I poked around a little. I noticed that the front door of the dressing room was off the hinges (leaving me vulnerable to my more unstable fans!). Also the toilet hadn't been cleaned in a long time. I wish I knew a forensics expert who could've told me exactly how long, but I would guess at least seven years. I was amused and forgiving about the dirty toilet (probably because they at least had a bottle of hand soap by the sink—I've made venues go buy soap for me). So we're standing around in this mess, waiting for the show to begin, when two guys with tool boxes appear from nowhere and proceed to *reattach the front door*. Gregg and I laughed. "You guys haven't found five minutes to scrub your toilet in the past seven years, but you found two guys to *reattach a door* at eight p.m. on a Monday night in Toledo?" That couldn't have been cheap. There must have been some sort of *after-hours door-hinge-replacement surcharge*. Now, that's not the kind of *big* story people like to hear, but it's an experience I'll remember for the rest of my life.

I was quite happy to get booked in Toledo. While I love doing shows in the big cities (New York City, Chicago, Cleveland), I also enjoy a good *secondary market* (Ithaca, Springfield, Akron). There's something about performing in a city where they don't expect to ever see you. They're appreciative. They say things like "Thank you for coming to Hattiesburg" as much as they say "Good show." And almost every town has their version of a hipster coffee shop, so I can hang out in a new city and still be in my comfort zone.

When I met with my book agent for the first time, I told him I wanted to write something, but I didn't have an idea. We talked for a bit, and I mentioned my love for performing in smaller cities. He said, "Why don't you write the book about that?"

Sounds good to me.

I wrote up a little treatment and a few weeks later, I had a book deal bigger than J. K. Rowling's and John Grisham's combined.

My original plan was to book one secondary-market show in all fifty states, in about a year, but thinking that would work was funnier than anything in my act. I would've been away for at least six months. Also getting a gig in Wyoming isn't easy. Not everything in my life needs to be practical, but that plan was just too ambitious.

So, instead of all fifty states in a year, my agent booked multiple shows in *a lot of* states, plus Israel and Canada.

Thank You for Coming to Hattiesburg is part tour diary and part memoir. It's chock-full of juicy details guaranteed to *deglamorize* your preconceptions about life on the road. There's also a chance it could glamorize them.

I'd love to tell you more, but I need to go book a flight to Evansville, Indiana.

JUANITA'S CANTINA

On January 14, 2015, I opened for Louis C.K. in front of fourteen thousand people at Madison Square Garden. Five days later I was on a plane headed to Little Rock, Arkansas, to headline a show at Juanita's Cantina, the first stop on my never-officially-titled "Secondary Markets Tour."

It amused me that I'd just done a show in a sold-out arena and was now on my way to perform at a small music venue in Little Rock. But I'm realistic; I could never fill Madison Square Garden. And now might be a good time to mention that I didn't even fill Juanita's Cantina.

This was my second time performing at Juanita's. I did a show there in 2008, when they were at a different location. About ninety people showed up on a Tuesday. I remember thinking afterward, *Ninety people on a Tuesday in Little Rock. Not bad!* Although I've always toured, I still spend most of my time in New York City, so the fact that nearly a hundred people would pay to see me in Little Rock was pretty satisfying.

But then I think, *Maybe if I* wasn't *satisfied with ninety people in Little Rock, I'd be playing the Little Rock equivalent of Madison Square Garden.* Right?

I arrived the night before the show. I would've preferred to arrive earlier in the day, but the only nonstop flight to Little Rock was at 6:00 p.m. After touring for twenty-seven years, you start coming up with some travel *dealbreakers*, and one of mine is booking a flight with a layover when a nonstop is available. Another dealbreaker: a hotel where the door opens to the outside.

I did a tiny bit of research before I arrived. I asked my friend Jeremy, a comedy producer from New York who used to live in Little Rock, to recommend some places to check out. He not only e-mailed me an extensive list of restaurants, bars, and museums, but he even included links. Not links under the name of the place, but links where you click on the name of the place and its website appears. If I ever do this for you it means you saved my life once or I'm in love with you.

I arrived around 8:30 p.m. My stomach was a bit upset, so I figured the best thing to do was go to the bar next to the hotel and get some chicken fingers with "voodoo" sauce and a glass of Pinot Noir. This *pairing* is also known as "the upset stomach's best friend."

The next morning I dove into my favorite on-the-road activity: finding a coffee shop that makes me feel like I'm in Brooklyn. Going to coffee shops is probably my favorite part of traveling. I'll go on Yelp to search coffee shops that are near a hotel I'm not staying at for six weeks. In Little Rock, a place called Mylo came highly recommended, and when I read a Yelp review where a guy complained that the barista there wouldn't grind a bag of beans he was buying because you should only grind coffee beans right before making the coffee, I knew this was the place for me.

Mylo wasn't within walking distance, so I got an Uber. A male driver arrived with a woman in the passenger seat. She stuck her head out the window and said, "Todd?" I got in, and the driver smiled and said, "This is my wife. She's also an Uber driver." Then he pointed to both of their licenses mounted above the windshield. Getting picked up by a husband-and-wife Uber team was a delightful start to my morning.

Mylo was great. The type of place I'd stay at for hours with the intention of getting work done, but then I wouldn't get any work done. And as I suspected, everyone there was extremely friendly, and no, not because they recognized me from the one minute, eight seconds I was in the movie *Pootie Tang*. No one recognized me. *Believe* me, if someone recognized me there, you would've heard about it by now (and there will be that kind of thing if you keep reading!). I sat at Mylo and did a little research about the neighborhood I was in, an artsy community called Hillcrest. I put "Hillcrest" into my little Android browser and found something called "the Shoppes on Woodlawn," which looked like it was in a house around the corner. It seemed like a place to get my girlfriend a gift from the road. I liked to buy her little gifts when I went out of town. Often they weren't very imaginative, like a refrigerator magnet from Alaska that just said "AK." (Treated myself to one, too!)

There was a very friendly man at the front desk of the Shoppes. I asked if there was anything "Arkansas-specific" to buy as a gift. He showed me some sort of tree ornaments shaped like Arkansas. I didn't know how my girlfriend could use such an item, and I wasn't going to buy her a tree to go with it, so I left empty-handed.

When you go to Little Rock, everyone tells you to go to the Clinton Library. I'd been on my last trip but figured it was something I needed to do every time I came to town. The visit started out right. I was in line waiting for my admission sticker. An old man had just gotten his. He handed one to his wife and told her, "The woman at the counter said you're supposed to stick it on your forehead." It was such a simple, silly, perfect joke.

I saw a sign for a guided tour that started in a few minutes. *Hmmm. A guided tour? That's probably a good way to get some knowledge stuffed into my head that I wouldn't find on my own, but what about the* guided *part? Am I really a* guided *tour* guy? *I'd like to be, but what if the guide is long-winded? I can't focus on a conversation for more than thirty seconds. Okay. Let's do it.* The crowd for the tour was basically a sweet group of senior citizens from a local Baptist church and me, a very young Jewish man. The tour started out *slow*, like "Todd, get ready for a panic attack" slow. At the rate we were going, I couldn't imagine the tour lasting less than eleven hours, or maybe it was only scheduled for one hour and the tour guide would have to make everyone sprint through the last fifteen minutes. That could be fun. I'm a *completist* (I never walk out of movies) but this pace tortured me, so I gathered up some strength and *disengaged* from the group. There's a good chance the tour is still in progress.

I spent the next twenty minutes wandering around the museum looking for the slight mention of the whole Monica Lewinsky/impeachment thing that I found the last time I was in town. I got overwhelmed by the *text-heavy* displays, so I left before I found it.

I think I did a good job entertaining the fifty-eight people who showed up at Juanita's that night (yes, thirty-two fewer than my last trip). It wasn't the best-publicized show in town (I had to teach the promoter how to retweet), and I wasn't expecting a thousand people, but I bet I could've gotten a hundred fifty. You're supposed to get more people the second time you come through a city.

After the show, my opening act, Kris Pierce, invited me to a showcase for local comics at a bar a few miles away. I wasn't feeling great, but this is something I actually love doing—a short, no-pressure unpaid set after doing a higher-stakes paid headlining set. In New York, people like Chris Rock and Jerry Seinfeld will do unannounced *drop-in* sets at the comedy clubs. The crowd always goes apeshit. I imagined this is what it would be like if I did a set at an open mic in Little Rock. I'd be introduced and there would be a palpable sense of "Oh my God! I knew Todd Barry was in town and was hoping he'd do a set here, but I didn't think he would!" energy in the air. I defused this energy by showing up after the show ended.

Before I went to Little Rock I posted something about it on Facebook. Below it a woman commented, *Tough crowd for your quick clever wit*. She posted this *before* the show. In her mind she was giving me a compliment. She saw "Little Rock" and assumed everyone there was a redneck and that it would be a tough show. It wasn't a "tough crowd" (and you mean-spirited readers out there are saying it wasn't a *crowd* at all). I've had this happen when I promote shows in other regions that aren't in big markets. I remember posting a list of my upcoming tour dates on Instagram (yes, you can do that) that included two dates in North Dakota and one in South Dakota. A woman commented, *Living the dream*. I'm guessing she was being sarcastic. I doubt she would've said this if my tour dates were Chicago, San Francisco, and New York. I didn't respond to the comment, but I would've liked to yell at her, "WHAT DREAM ARE YOU LIVING?!" That would have *annihilated* her.

I saw in the paper that singer/songwriter Randy Newman had a show in Little Rock with a local orchestra the same night as mine. The next morning I spotted him on my flight from Little Rock to Dallas. This is the second time I've been on a flight with Randy Newman. I left him alone, but it might have been fun to talk to him:

"Sorry to bother you, Mr. Newman, but this is the second time I've been on a flight with you, so I think that makes it okay. I did a show in Little Rock last night, too. I'm a comedian."

He'd reply, "Oh, great. How was your show?"

"Pretty good, but there were only fifty-eight people there. I'm guessing your show was sold out."

He would shrug politely, then say, "I had more than fifty-eight people in my orchestra."

Brief pause.

"Well, next time I'll return with an orchestra!"

We'd both laugh and I'd walk back to my seat in coach.

ACM PERFORMANCE LAB

I was brought to Oklahoma City by a collective of comedians called OKC Comedy. These guys do comedy and also produce shows with national headliners. This was the second time they'd brought me there. You might think being booked by another comedian must be a good thing—they know how they like to be treated and treat you the same— but that's not always the case. If a comic produces a show, there's always a chance that they're bitter because they can't make enough money performing, and they end up bullying or just flat-out ripping off other comics.

The OKC Comedy guys were great. They liked getting some of their comedy heroes down to Oklahoma City, with the added benefit that they got to open the shows. You can only imagine the power of having "Opened for Todd Barry" on your résumé. It pretty much assures your career is a "lock."

The first time I was there, in 2010, they met me at my hotel with a little gift basket. It included some candy and a $25 Chili's gift card. This kind of gesture doesn't happen very often and is always appreciated. I quickly ate the candy, but the Chili's card posed a slight challenge. I live in New York City, not exactly *Chili's territory*. And I probably wouldn't go to Chili's on the road (because of my passion for supporting mom-and-pop businesses). So I was walking around with a wallet that was already too thick with coffee shop punch cards and at least one SAG card. (Why not have the current one and the one from the previous quarter, just to prove your longevity in the acting world? Also, in all the acting jobs I've done, I've never been asked to show my SAG card.) I eventually cashed the Chili's card at an airport location, which freed up space for a third SAG card.

One of the local comics, Cameron Buchholtz, was nice enough to show me around a few times during my two-day visit. He took me to get an "onion burger," an Oklahoma specialty I'd seen featured on one of the food networks, possibly even the actual Food Network. This is a burger where a huge handful of onions is mixed in with the meat, probably a 1:1 ratio. We went to a place called Tucker's. It turns out an onion burger is exactly what it sounds like. Delicious, but not a lot of surprises. If you're waiting for my great "onion burger story," it's not gonna happen.

The show was at the Academy of Contemporary Music Performance Lab at the University of Central Oklahoma, which usually hosts events like Zappa Plays Zappa (Dweezil Zappa playing songs by his late father, Frank). I played to what we call in the business a "capacity crowd." Not sold out, but full. I was the first comic to perform there, which means they worked some of the kinks out with me, enabling future comedians to have a *safe haven* to perform. At my show they learned that next time they should serve drinks in plastic cups—there was quite a bit of bottle clanking, which is a problem for a guy like me, who's in the business of serving up *soft-spoken gems*.

My favorite memory of the trip is driving around with Cameron and passing a building under construction. It looked like railroad cars stacked up on top of each other in a crisscross pattern, like the way a pretentious bistro stacks their french fries (I'm sorry, *frites*). If he told me it was a replica of I. M. Pei's weekend home, I would've believed him. "What is *that*?" I asked.

"That's going to be a corn dog restaurant."

"Really?"

"Yes."

I'll be back.

Future corn dog restaurant. Oklahoma City.

SALLY TOMATOES

It's rare that I get booked in a city I've never even heard of, so I'm surprised I didn't do more research on Rohnert Park, a city forty miles north of San Francisco. From the little bit I'd done, I got the feeling it was going to have a *Silicon Valley* vibe, or perhaps a *wine country* vibe. If you asked me to give a specific description of either of those *vibes* I would probably give you a gentle sneer and say, "C'mon, you know what I mean." When I actually arrived I updated my description to *Boca Raton vibe*. That was solely based on seeing a golf course and some low-rise, nondescript buildings. (I actually spent two semesters at Florida Atlantic University in Boca Raton, so I guess it was a somewhat *informed* assessment.)

The next day one of the local opening comics, a friendly guy named Steve Ausburne, offered to drive me around a bit.

"What goes on in Rohnert Park?" I asked.

He shook his head. "You know, I start to tell people about it and I get bored," he responded.

He suggested taking me to Santa Rosa, a nearby town that was a bit more *happening*. We went to a coffee shop there, and because it had white walls, I concluded that it had a *Charleston vibe*.

My show that night was in a complex called the SOMO Village Event Center. Everything was dark while we were headed there. It seemed like we were driving on service roads, and I never got the feeling of "Ooh, we're about to reach the *entertainment district*." We arrived at the complex. It was very warehouselike. I couldn't get a feel for what even went on there. It felt like some sort of community rec center. There was a group of guys playing darts in what seemed like an informal league, a snack bar, and the nightclub I was performing at, Sally Tomatoes. As a comic, I was used to playing comedy clubs with silly names (In 2001 I played two different clubs with "Banana" in the name). This time I was happy about the name because it gave me another chance to use this obvious opening line: "A couple of weeks ago I opened for Louis C.K. at Madison Square Garden, so I'm pretty excited to be playing Sally Tomatoes . . ." There was an eruption of laughs and it turned out to be a fun show, in a weird room that seemed like a banquet hall.

I didn't bring any merch (what we call *merchandise* in show business) to sell on this trip. (If you want to seem like a showbiz insider, say things like "I wonder if the band is selling any *merch*" next time you go to a concert.) But I still did an informal little *meet-and-greet*, meaning I stood in the hall by the dressing room door, groveling for "That was great"s and "You were funny"s. If I were a bigger comic playing big theaters, I could sell separate, higher-priced tickets that included a meet-and-greet, and I would get paid to meet my fans and get extra compliments. But at my level, I do it for free. And my fans are so great I'd pay THEM—never mind.

After shaking a few hands at Sally Tomatoes I saw a familiar smiling face approach me: Metallica drummer Lars Ulrich. I'm not a huge fan of heavy metal, but I am a *colossal* fan of meeting famous people. No one is more starstruck than a celebrity. When you see some celeb hanging out with another celebrity and you wonder what they have in common, it's mainly that they're just celebrities.

Lars was a very friendly guy and, as it turns out, a huge Todd Barry fan. He told me he listened to my albums with his teenage son. He quoted jokes of mine that I'd forgotten about. People caught on he was there and started asking him for pictures. He obliged but made sure to include me, so I didn't get upstaged at my own show.

During one of these pictures I had one of those "Why did I say that?" moments. We were posing with a mutual fan when I felt the need to ask Lars, "What's your son's name?" What a weird, dumb question. *What's your son's name?* It's not like he was wheeling the kid in a baby stroller at my show. His son wasn't even with him. He did introduce me to his glamorous and friendly fiancée. I imagined Lars asking her, "Baby, you want to go see Todd Barry tonight? The comedian who does the joke about trying to buy a wallet at Old Navy. He's playing some place I've never even heard of. I'll Google Maps it." He asked me how the Madison Square Garden show went. I realized he probably approaches a show there the way I would a small club.

Eventually the pictures and chitchat stopped, and we said our good-byes.

We never talked music, so I didn't get a chance to tell him about the ten hours of Belle and Sebastian music on my iTunes.

Lars Ulrich and me. Rohnert Park, California.

FEBRUARY 13 AND 14, 2015—TRAVERSE CITY, MICHIGAN

TRAVERSE CITY WINTER COMEDY ARTS FESTIVAL

I flew Delta to Traverse City because their flights are routed through Detroit, which meant, according to the festival promoters, they were less likely to get canceled due to weather than flights via Chicago, which would've been on United, my PREFERRED airline. It's not my PREFERRED airline because it's better, I just have accumulated more frequent-flier miles with them, and therefore have PREMIER GOLD STATUS with them. I know I'm hitting a few points HARD, but this stuff is important to me. You get STATUS with an airline by hitting various mileage thresholds (you fly twenty-five thousand miles in a year, you get Silver status). Get a couple of touring comics together and bring up the topic of frequent-flier miles, and watch their eyes light up. Although I love talking about frequent-flier miles, I've been on many flights and overheard more traditional *businessman*-type guys in first class talking about them, and all I think is, *Wow, what shallow awful people*. They'll start talking to each other without any introduction, the way men will talk to strangers about sports. They often complain about the frequent-flier program itself: "I remember when it *meant* something to be Delta Diamond Medallion status. Now I can't always get an upgrade on a flight to Pittsburgh."

So I got on the smallish plane and I sat down in my aisle seat—the same aisle seat I *chose* online, *in advance*. Two women boarded the plane and one of them muttered something about having a middle seat. She turned to me and asked, "Would you switch seats? I have bad knees."

"To a middle seat?" I said, like she asked me to sit on the floor. She nodded yes. I'd been asked to switch seats before. Usually it's a family or couple that got separated, and you move from one aisle seat to another, and you feel like a great guy. This was different. She was asking me to go from a precious aisle seat to the most hated seat on the plane. Even people who aren't FFs (frequent fliers) don't want middle seats. I'm sure everyone around me was rooting for me, thinking, *Hold your ground, buddy. That's an unreasonable request.* But she triggered my oversensitive guilt mechanism, so I thought about it for a few seconds, taking into consideration her "bad knees," and moved over. I'm sure I did a few subtle, incredulous headshakes and huffs and puffs as I sat down. After sitting there a few minutes, I realized the "I have bad knees" thing was something I was just supposed to accept without thinking about it. I looked at the legroom I had and the amount she had: the middle seat has the same amount of legroom as the aisle. So unless she was going to stretch her legs out and block the path of the flight attendants, she'd have been just as comfortable in the middle seat. Why didn't I think of this when she asked? I let myself get hoodwinked and/or flimflammed! But the flight was just a little over an hour—not a long time to sit in a middle seat, seething because you just took the high road.

This was my second trip to the Traverse City Winter Comedy Arts Festival, presented by filmmaker Michael Moore and comedian Jeff Garlin. It's different from other comedy festivals because it's not in a big city and it's mainly about the comedy. Some festivals attract a lot of agents, managers, or "development" people from TV networks, so there's a tendency to worry about "who was in the room" when you were onstage. There isn't a strong *industry* presence at this festival, so you can relax a bit.

I first came to this festival in 2013. They were nice enough to include two plane tickets in the deal so I could bring my girlfriend. Usually you have to go *out of pocket* if you want to bring a date.

We checked into the hotel and were given an accessible room for the disabled. I've stayed in these rooms before—sometimes they're offered with the incentive that they're "bigger." Usually there are just rails in the shower and other minor changes to make things easier for someone in a wheelchair. But this room was different. It had all the rails, but it also had a huge medical contraption on a shelf. It wasn't a wheelchair; it was some type of sling. I wish I'd taken a picture of it, but at the same time, I know why I didn't. Whatever it was, it made me feel like I was staying in a hospital room.

Ted Alexandro was on my flight for the 2015 festival. Ted's a really funny comedian and a good friend. We were both staying at the same hotel, a different one than the one I'd stayed at the previous time. I'm always excited by a new hotel, and I'd found the one I stayed in last time to be depressing. What I didn't know is that the original hotel was overbooked, so Ted and I were the only comedians staying at the new hotel, which was in the middle of nowhere. Part of the fun of festivals is getting to hang out with your friends, a nice break from the typical lonely road gig. You can run into people in the lobby and there's always a familiar face (or a face you should remember but don't).

I asked Ted, "Should we try to move to the other hotel? I don't want to say in this area. It's depressing." Ted agreed.

I asked the driver to check if any rooms had opened up at that other place. They had, so we checked out of the hotel and got back in the van. Didn't feel bad about it. It's not like when you go to a restaurant, sit down, look at the menu, and realize you don't want to eat there, then leave. I always feel bad about that.

The downside of the festival is that it's freezing in Michigan in February. It was extra cold this trip (even the locals were saying this), so I didn't explore as much as I would have liked. I did go to a coffee shop

I'd discovered on a previous trip called Morsels (my favorite name for any business I've ever patronized). Like every single person in Traverse City, the people who worked there were extremely friendly, and the shop had something I'd never seen before: a little file by the cash register for people to store their punch cards. I'm not sure what the motivation was to build that. Were people losing their cards and the owners just said, "Hey, just keep it here! Fuck it, we'll build a rack"? I bet if I lived there they'd let me use it to store my SAG card.

My show with Ted started at nine thirty, so we had time to check out Michael Moore's solo show at a different venue. Michael had just tweeted something about snipers not being heroes, so security was tight. We had to walk through a metal detector before we sat down, and there were secret-service-type guys scattered about. This was a quaint little playhouse, so those metal detectors had to be rentals. I couldn't imagine there was a metal detector rental place in Traverse City. Maybe they had to be shipped. Yikes. Think of the postage and handling charges! Luckily for Michael, the audience was filled with people who agreed with everything he said, so there were no incidents.

Security was a little less tight at my show with Ted. He was on before me, and I felt a wave of nervousness. Normally I wouldn't be nervous to follow Ted, and that's not an insult. I've been able to follow all sorts of acts in my career (including a guy in Long Island who ended with a reggae bit where he attached fake dreadlocks). Sometimes an act is "hard to follow" because they're bad, or just not a good fit with the whole show (I didn't expect to have a good set after the dreadlocks guy). Or a comic whose act is stupid, full of shallow observations, and delivered with a big smile and a fake laugh—or even a comic who performs with genuine enthusiasm—that might set a tone that makes it rough for a super-intellectual/brainiac/academic comic like myself to follow. I guess I'm saying I can't follow any comic. But seriously, it can be a compliment to be a comic who is easy to follow. It means they set a thoughtful tone and get people listening instead of getting them stirred up. But I was still nervous and put it in my head that it was going to be rough.

So Ted goes on and is doing very well. His material is sharp, and he has an organic, likable presence. The crowds at this festival skew older, and the theater wasn't full, so they wouldn't be described as *pumped*. But he was doing well enough and I just put myself in a bad headspace and went on to have a mediocre set. The jokes were *landing*, but there was some *dead air*. Not awful, but not good or fun.

The next night I had a co-headlining set with Doug Benson, a comic I've known forever who is very famous for his pot consumption. One of my earliest memories of Doug happened at the Sunset Marquis hotel in Los Angeles, at least twenty years ago. I have no idea why I was in this hotel lobby with Doug, but I do remember that we spotted Jean-Claude Van Damme at the front desk checking in. Doug said hi to him, then, before I knew it, put his hands up and started *air-boxing* him. Making a "let's fight" joke to Jean-Claude Van Damme is like meeting a comedian and saying, "Say something funny." But JCVD was a good sport. He made a "Whoa, I'm scared" gesture, put his fists up, and played along.

This show was at the City Opera House. I looked at their schedule of events. Didn't see a lot of operas. But it feels great getting to say you're doing a show at an opera house, and this show had a *looser* feel and was way more fun than the previous night.

Everyone who worked at this festival was so friendly that I told someone it made me feel uncomfortable. Shortly after I said this I was sitting with some comics. One of them said, "Everyone is so nice here it makes me uncomfortable." This was sincere sweetness we were feeling. I never felt I would be asked to join a cult. It was a good kind of uncomfortable. Not middle seat uncomfortable.

FEBRUARY 21, 2015—BETHLEHEM, PENNSYLVANIA
STEELSTACKS

I got to Bethlehem the day before the show. I drove from New York with my opening act, Doogie Horner, who I met when he opened for me in Philadelphia. When I asked him if he wanted to do the gig he told me he was from Bethlehem. This made me feel good, like I was giving him a paid trip home. We stopped at a McDonald's in White-house Station, New Jersey, a city I'd never heard of. I've done hundreds of shows in New Jersey, and I still don't understand the geography. All I know is that Hoboken and Jersey City are pretty close to Manhattan. This was a particularly interesting McDonald's—*I bet it wasn't, Todd*—really small, and stuck on the end of a strip mall. I ordered one of their Chicken Snack Wraps, which are pretty good (and priced to sell!). I usually get these with barbecue sauce, but at this tiny place, they only offered ranch. Now, I *can* eat ranch, but I'm not ever gonna order ranch. I asked very politely, "You only have ranch?" Yep. Scaled-down McDonald's has a scaled-down sauce selection.

I didn't want to get filled up because Doogie had told me about a hot dog place called Yocco's, which sounded great. I liked every topping on their signature hot dog: mustard, onion, and some sort of chili sauce. Usually when a restaurant has some sort of *signature* sandwich, there are a few toppings that aren't going to work for me, and I feel like I'm compromising everything they stand for by ordering my way.

While driving to Pennsylvania I got a call from my doctor—more specifically, my gastroenterologist. He'd left a message a few days prior to discuss the results of an ultrasound I'd had because I was having some abdominal pain.

On the message he mentioned finding a small cholesterol polyp and that my liver was a bit fatty, but that this could be taken care of with a little weight loss and that I should have another ultrasound in a year. I basically understood the message, but I had questions, and I also like the challenge of getting a doctor to return a phone call, so I'd rung him up before I left. He called back during the drive and used the phrase "for all intents and purposes, your ultrasound was normal."

I wanted to be careful, so when we got to Yocco's I just had one hot dog. It wasn't until we arrived in Bethlehem that I took the phrase "for all intents and purposes, your ultrasound was normal" as my cue to run wild.

Hot dog. Yocco's. Allentown, Pennsylvania.

I checked into a bed-and-breakfast called the Sayre Mansion. I haven't stayed in many bed-and-breakfasts, but this is the place where the venue chose to put me, and I found glowing reviews on Trip-Advisor, and it seemed like it would have more character than the usual chain hotel. I liked the place. There was a nice woman at the front desk and a cute little dog named Lola. The woman walked me up a flight of stairs to my room. She returned a few minutes later when I realized I couldn't figure out how to turn on the TV. I'm embarrassed that I was even thinking about complaining about the TV in a bed-and-breakfast, but, you know, I have to watch *Masterpiece Theatre*!

A blizzard was headed toward Bethlehem, but I was assured by Doogie, who had talked to the promoter, that the show was going to happen.

I did a fairly exhaustive Yelp search to find a place to eat. I sorted by *distance* at first (a *pro move* on my part), but it was too cold to walk anywhere. Doogie was going to eat with his parents—he invited me to join them, but in a way that (correctly) implied *I know you probably won't want to eat with me and my parents.* I'm pretty good about eating alone—I've even done podcast interviews on the subject—and when you're a touring comic, you really have no choice sometimes. It's not that I *love* eating alone, it's more like I'm glad I don't have a problem with it.

I found a place called the Bethlehem Star Cafe. It had a solid four-star Yelp rating, and more important, I got a good *vibe* from it.

As much as I'm comfortable eating alone, and as much as I sort of *wanted* to eat alone, I had something else to consider: it was a Friday night. I had no idea what that meant in Bethlehem, Pennsylvania, but I was worried about sitting alone in a place that was packed and getting stared at by people who weren't alone. So I invited Doogie. He's a good guy, and he ate early enough with his folks that he could still join me.

I'm usually pretty sporty with my opening acts—I will pay for their meals, especially if they're driving me around—but I have to say that I was a bit excited that Doogie had already eaten and was probably going to order something small, or maybe just a drink.

I guess he was still a little peckish from his dinner with his parents, because he ordered a steak.

But he drove me around, so that's fine (I guess). I ordered something called huli-huli chicken. I'd never heard of huli-huli chicken. It was just a grilled chicken breast with some sort of soy-based sauce on it served with rice and snap peas. I was surprised I'd never heard of it since I eat so much Asian food. I found out later it's actually a Hawaiian dish. I love simple food. If the waiter describes an item on the menu and it has, like, three ingredients, I get excited the way people get excited about truffles.

I found an intriguing bar for after dinner called the Bookstore Speakeasy. I'm a big fan of the speakeasy-type bars that are popping up all over the country. I realize none of the speakeasies I've been to are actually speakeasies—I've never sat in one worried that it will get raided by the Bureau of Prohibition—but that doesn't matter. I like the subtle signage and multiple ice options.

The next day I got word from the promoter that the snow was so heavy, they needed to cancel the show after all. For the most part I'm a traditional "show must go on" type of guy, especially if I already traveled hours to be there, but the promoter mentioned that the venue had a policy where they only gave refunds if the show was actually canceled. So if I chose to do the show, anyone who didn't feel like traveling (or more likely was unable to travel) in a blizzard would not get a refund. Seemed like a weird policy to me, but I knew that if someone couldn't get a refund they'd blame me, so I agreed to the cancellation and the promoter rebooked me immediately.

Rather than spending the night, Doogie and I drove back to beat the storm. But I'll be back soon, Bethlehem. Start warming up the huli-huli sauce!

THE COMEDY ATTIC

Let's start with an exciting UPDATE. Or more like a CORREC-TION: Earlier, like maybe five seconds ago, when talking about my trip to Bethlehem, Pennsylvania, I told a wonderful story about going to a tiny McDonald's where they only had one choice of sauce for my chicken wrap. In my elitist mind, I assumed this was due to the size of the McDonald's. Well, on the way to Bloomington, Indiana, I went through the drive-through at a much larger McDonald's and was told about the "ranch only" policy—it was the new default sauce. One of the most humiliating experiences of the tour so far. But also one of the most interesting!

This was my third trip to Bloomington. Each time, I've played the same club. The first time it was part of the Funny Bone chain, then the owner, Jared, broke away and changed it to the Comedy Attic. I was put up at some sort of compound, although technically it was a hotel. There wasn't anything around it, so I asked Jared why he chose this place. He said, "I know comics like to be isolated, so I thought this would be good." Comics like to be isolated? When did that start? Comics like to be able to walk to get coffee and food. Jared also made a curious suggestion for a promotional poster, which was forwarded as a jpeg by my management before I got to town. It was a shot of me with a burning cityscape in the background. I opened the e-mail I and was mortified. *What do you suppose I'm going to think about when I see skyscrapers on fire?* A few years had elapsed since 9/11, and maybe I'm extra sensitive because I live in New York (and I realize my comedy is so powerful it starts fires) but I had them change it to something tamer.

Burning cityscape poster.

I eventually warmed up to Jared. He's a good guy, a true comedy fan, and he runs a really tight ship. A lot of comedy clubs pay lip service to shitty audience behavior: they'll make an announcement saying, "Put your phones on vibrate and keep your table talk to a minimum." (The "put your phones on vibrate" line is left over from the time when you couldn't text or tweet and all you were worried about was a phone ringing. This needs to be updated to "Don't use your phones at all.") This announcement is often said over a Blues Brothers song, so people don't necessarily take it in. But Jared does a more severe preemptive warning.

Before the show he plays a video (starring him) where he mentions that *USA Today* named his club one of the top ten in the country, followed by:

> *Some of you out there might be first-timers, so we'd like to point out a couple of things that make a show go great. Don't let your cell phone interrupt the show with texting or letting it ring, and most importantly be cool. Please do not heckle or comment on jokes. It's a long-standing misconception that comedians want you to heckle or yell out to try to help the show. Well, they don't want you to do that, and it won't help. If for some reason you thought you were one of those people who thought you'd try to add to the show—talk, yell out—it's not a big deal, it's not for everybody, we just ask you to exit the show quietly. I honestly believe these simple guidelines are the number one reason we're top ten in the country. So let's sit back, relax, and laugh loud. And welcome to the Comedy Attic.*

It's an intense way to start the show—especially the part where he tells potential hecklers to quietly leave. But it's effective: I've never had an incident there, and it *is* considered one of the best clubs in the country.

One of the things that comics mention when talking about the Comedy Attic is the communal greenroom, which is actually the office in the back of the club. You might be in there alone, or you might be in there while Jared is watching TV with one of his kids. I probably could've said, "Hey, Jared, brother, could you give me a little alone time, I want to cleanse my negative thoughts so I can do a great show," but I didn't. I hung out in the office and talked to him.

I never told Jared about a practical joke I played on him after my first trip to Bloomington. I asked him if he knew a good place to get coffee. He responded with a defiant, "Dunkin' Donuts coffee is the only kind I like." He said this with the urgency of someone who had a gun to his head, like I was sent there by the Dunkin' people to test his loyalty. So when I returned to the club the next time with Neil Hamburger and Brendon Walsh, I told them, "One of us has to ask Jared for a coffee recommendation. *Trust me.*" I felt guilty even suggesting this because I'm not a big prank guy, but I let myself do it. So when we were all together someone asked, "Hey, Jared, do you know a good place to get coffee?"

He very politely answered, "I'm not a big coffee drinker. I think there are a few cafés around."

I was mortified. *C'mon, Jared, do the "I only drink Dunkin' Donuts coffee" thing. You just fucked up the weakest prank in history!*

I didn't tell him about this, but we did talk movies, specifically the annual list Jared makes (and posts on Facebook) of the best movies he saw in the last year. I disagreed vehemently with his top choice. I realize I'm supposed to tell you the title, but I don't want to burn any bridges with the film industry. But if you are the director of this film and figure out I'm talking to you (and you were thinking of putting me in your next film), just know that I'm all about second chances.

THE DROP COMEDY CLUB

I first played South Bend in 2002. I did eight shows over six nights at the Funny Bone. Part of the reason I try to avoid comedy clubs when I tour now is that I end up getting booked for eight shows over six nights in a city the size of South Bend, where there really isn't that kind of demand for me.

I was picked up at the airport by the owner, who, on the drive to my hotel, confessed, "The only thing I'm worried about is that you'll be too smart for my audiences." I took that as a compliment, and also as a comforting acknowledgment: "I'm aware this might not go well. I only have myself to blame for booking you."

It did not go well. And not because I was "too smart" for the audiences (but if I did think that I wouldn't tell you). I had a few decent shows but also bombed a few times during the week. I even got a sweet message on my website's message board (this was 2002) saying I "didn't have a leg to stand on."

But there were surprising moments, too. Whenever I talk with other comics about getting dirty looks from audience members, I refer to one of the eight South Bend shows I had in 2002. There was a woman right up front who had the biggest sneer on her face during my show. When this happens I try to turn away from the unsatisfied person in favor of someone who's enjoying themselves. But sometimes you just have to pivot back and *check in* with the unhappy person to see if you've turned things around, and also to torture yourself. I checked in a few times with this woman, and it seemed like she wasn't having it. She'd made a huge mistake when she bought tickets (or more likely got free passes) for my show. She was *angry.*

So the show ended, and it was time for my favorite part of the evening: selling CDs to an audience that didn't enjoy me. I laid copies of my seminal *Medium Energy* CD, which I self-released, punk-rock-style, out on a table and stood there. The previously mentioned angry woman, still maintaining that hateful, dissatisfied look, walked up. I thought, *Here it comes.* She looked me in the eye and said, "Give me *four.* I just got my tax refund." I don't remember what I said to her, but it was probably along the lines of "Wow, I thought you hated me." You know, something *smooth.* But I realized she just had one of those "I hate you" faces, so I took her forty bucks and handed her four CDs. This is more than I'd ever sold to any one person. I can't imagine where those CDs ended up. Hopefully they went to the South Bend library.

I returned in 2008 to do a show at Notre Dame. College shows are a real crapshoot because you don't know what to expect. It can be five thousand drunk kids in an auditorium during "Parents Weekend" or my favorite scenario: fifty nerdy kids show up because they had nothing to do that night.

I was nervous about playing Notre Dame because it's a religious school. I'm not the dirtiest comic (probably PG-13) but you never know what's going to offend someone. I was relieved when I walked into the student union and saw a meeting of a gay student group going on. I thought, *Okay, this might be more relaxed than I thought.*

The show at Notre Dame turned out great. I didn't have the feeling I was performing for "kids." They got all my references and were enthusiastic. The only real problem was with a woman who was there to photograph the show. She'd asked beforehand if she could take some flash pictures. Without giving it too much thought, I said sure. I didn't realize that she would sit up front, and she'd take five hundred pictures in the first thirty seconds I was on stage. I'm not sure why she thought this *dance club atmosphere* was okay, but she was a nice young woman, so I gently told her it might be a bit distracting to deal with for forty-five minutes.

The Drop Comedy Club marquee. South Bend, Indiana.

For my 2015 trip, I scaled things down a bit. I did one show at a hundred-seater called the Drop Comedy Club. I drove there with opening act Josh Cocks, who told me a great story about an Indiana club owner who wouldn't consider booking him unless he changed his name. She said she had a "family-friendly" club and suggested he go by "Cox" (even though "Cocks" is his legal name). I arrived to find a place that looked like a seafood shack. The marquee was covered in Saran Wrap that just said "Comedy" and the hours they were open for breakfast. Two hundred yards away stood the St. Joseph County Jail. It was so close, it would've been an ideal place for an after-party. (Although I went online and saw that it had a 2.5 Google rating. Seriously.)

My comedian friend Andy Kindler once said something I related to: "Give me a nice half-full room." I think part of the reason I'm not a huge star is that playing a hundred-seater sounds great to me, and you get that "half-full" looseness even when it's full.

Inside the place was everything I hoped for. There was a separate bar, and then the "showroom" in the back, where one hundred chairs were laid out nice and tight in a semicircle. It had a secretive vibe to it, like it would be a good place to organize a protest for the opening of a Walmart. The tight seating made it easy to work the crowd. Had some good banter with a guy up front. I think it involved my guessing that he was an engineer. After the show I was talking to this guy at the merch table when a young man approached and asked, "Where do you guys go next?" I was confused for a moment, then laughed when I realized he thought the guy was a *plant*—as in, like, he's an improv actor who tours with me and pretends he's an engineer, so we can have that magical two-minute moment. People think any spontaneous moment at a comedy show is set up. I had one at Caroline's in

New York recently. I asked a woman what neighborhood she lived in. She said the Upper East Side. I said, "That's a great place to live if you like hanging out with podiatrists." She said, "I'm a podiatrist." She wasn't a *plant*, either. I don't need *plants* to be funny. I wish I could afford a plant.

MARCH 17, 2015—ASHEVILLE, NORTH CAROLINA

THE GREY EAGLE

I'm probably someone who's used the phrase "I hate hippies" at least a hundred times in my life. I don't actually *hate* hippies, although when I see one I do feel hatred, so whatever you call the combination of feeling hatred without actually hating, that's how I feel about hippies. If I meet one and they're friendly and smart, I will forgive their ridiculous haircut, their tie-dyed shirt, their little satchel that holds their dumb hand-rolled cigarettes, and the excruciating music they listen to back at the house they share with nine other people. Asheville is full of good-natured hippies. I noticed this on my first trip there years ago. They came to my shows and laughed when I said things like, "This seems like an easy city to get laid in if you're a swami." They also quite enjoyed the mere mention of the eighty-year-old guy I saw walking around with a rain stick.

I arrived a day before the 2015 show. As I walked around Asheville I had an instant feeling of "Ooh, I would come here on vacation," followed by fantasizing about living there. When I'm on the road I often sit in my hotel room looking at real estate websites and saying, "Oh man, I could live like a *king* if I moved here."

My opening act was Minori Hinds, a funny young comic from Asheville I'd met on a previous visit. I texted her to meet for a drink. I didn't want to go to a loud or fratty bar. Minori mentioned a "gothic" bar, which I interpreted as "goth" bar, so I rejected that. Although I do have the Cure's *Pornography* album and the single "Friday I'm in Love" on my iTunes, I'm still about three months too old to go to a goth bar. She also suggested a place called the Rankin Vault. As we entered, the doorman looked at me and asked, "Are you a fucking actor?" He wasn't hostile, just one of those guys who peppers his conversation with a heaping amount of unnecessary of "fuck"s. I laughed in the stunned way you laugh when someone says something inappropriate. I said, "I'm more of a fucking comedian."

I ordered a burrito and a glass of wine. After a few minutes the doorman who wanted to know if I was a "fucking actor" walked up to me and said, "Hey, sorry about dropping that f-bomb, your first round is on me." I graciously accepted his apology, then even more graciously reminded the bartender about the arrangement when he started to charge me for that first round.

The day of the show I went to a coffee shop but wanted to see something a little more special, more local. Minori suggested checking out the Basilica of St. Lawrence, which was quite beautiful. I liked the idea of someone asking me later, "What did you do in Asheville in your free time?"

"Well, I grabbed some coffee and poked around a *basilica*."

"I'm sorry, what was that?" they'd ask.

"I assume you got the *coffee* part and it's the *basilica* thing that's freaking you out."

"Yeah, that caught me off guard."

I'd nod in an "I guess you don't really know me as well as you thought" way.

"Well. That sounds great. I'll have to check out a basilica if I ever go to Asheville," they would continue, knowing that *I know* they would never do something as cool and interesting as that.

I'm Jewish, but I like churches, and the basilica was beautiful. I walked inside and a shady-looking dude walked by me and asked if I had any questions. I didn't really have any questions, and part of me thought he didn't even work there. I crossed paths with him again as I was roaming around. This time I noticed he reeked of smoke. He asked me if I wanted to get a tour of the place. I was uncomfortable, so I left. I'm guessing he actually did work there, but I'm pretty sure he wasn't the *official tour guide*.

The Grey Eagle. Asheville, North Carolina.

Someone had tweeted a warning to me about Asheville audiences not shutting up during shows. I tweeted back, "That hasn't been my experience." Once again, the people who showed up were great. There was one dude who interrupted me a couple of times in an "I'm playing along" sort of way, but I politely shut him down, and then he eventually left, making me feel guilty, like I'd gone too far.

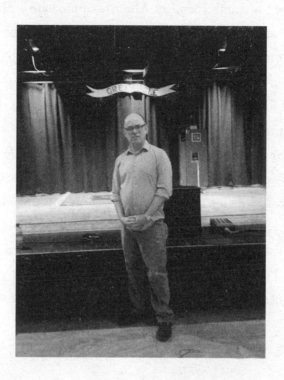

I'm a big fan of the *after-show hang*. I wanted to go to a bar, but it was St. Patrick's Day. I know what St. Patrick's Day is like in New York, and if it was even half as awful in Asheville then I needed to be careful. Minori said she was up for hanging out so we went for a little walk. I rejected the first bar we went to, even though it was empty. Then we walked by this place called the Crow and Quill, which had covered windows and an unmarked entrance. I'm a sucker for an *unmarked entrance*, so we went in. Turns out this was the aforementioned "gothic" bar, and it was just what I was looking for. It wasn't crazy loud, and it was a totally mixed crowd, young and old, "cool"-looking and uncool.

At some point I realized she meant it was a gothic bar in decor, and not full of people wearing lots of black eyeliner at the mall.

I had ordered a glass of their best "Goth Pinot Noir" and settled on a couch when a drunk friend of Minori's approached. She had been at the show and was complimentary at first, but then she started giving me *notes* on my act: "You should've talked about this more. You should've said this instead of this. . . ."

"Thanks for the input. I'm sorry I disappointed you. I will try to implement these changes shortly."

She didn't react so well to this, and things got a little tense. Normally I'd do what a therapist would recommend and *exit*, but I decided to see if I could defuse the tension as well as my own anger. I kept talking to her, asked her questions about her work as a chef. She shifted gears a bit; I eventually warmed up to her and we ended up hugging when I left. I'm not sure I'll always handle insults this way, but it was a nice experiment. Also, she probably had no idea she was insulting me.

MOTORCO MUSIC HALL

I drove to Durham with Minori, who had done a great job opening for me the previous night. She dropped me at my hotel and went to see a friend she was staying with. (If I'm doing a music venue, they don't usually pay for hotels, so I always pay for the opening act's room, although I *will* I ask them if they know someone they can stay with in the city we're playing, not because it saves me money on an extra hotel room, but because I'm passionate about helping people nurture and reignite fragile, neglected relationships.)

I felt a little uneasy heading to Durham because there wasn't a lot of breathing room between when I got there and showtime, and I was leaving the next day for Wilmington. I felt pressure to sightsee on some level, so I forced myself to take a walk in the mostly deserted downtown area. After walking about twelve minutes, I realized almost everything was closed, then headed back to the hotel to get ready for dinner with my friends Mac and Andrea. Mac is one of the founders of the band Superchunk as well as the Merge record label. Andrea owns a great restaurant in Chapel Hill called Lantern. They recommended eating at a pizza place called Toro. I'd heard Jerry Seinfeld ate there while he was in town, so I knew it was "comic-friendly." I'm from New York, where we have really good pizza, but I've never been one of those "You call this pizza? I'm from New York!" guys. I've had good pizza all over.

Mac and Andrea were a bit late. (I don't like when people are late, and if you are late meeting me, you risk getting called out in one of my bestselling books!) They arrived and I looked at the menu of fancy pizzas, searching for one with the fewest "dealbreaker" ingredients (e.g., mushrooms, whole tomatoes). A pizza jumped out at me. The ingredients: a cheese I'd never heard of, *two* kinds of onions, and pistachio nuts. That's right, TWO kinds of onions, and that's right again, pistachio nuts. I love onions, but I'd never think of putting two different types on any food. That's like me putting two kinds of punch lines in one of my jokes. I would've ordered it if it just had one type of onion. And pistachio nuts? Another thing I wouldn't have thought of putting on pizza. I can eat pistachio nuts until I'm sick.

I try not to get stuffed before a show, but in this case I couldn't help myself. I ate an entire pizza (give or take a slice I may have donated to Mac and Andrea). After dinner they drove me to the venue. It was at a rock club that was set up for a seated show. The promoter was a local comic named Debbie. She must have done a great job with publicity, because the place was packed. Minori opened with a strong set, which made me feel good. I want my audiences to like my opening act. I feel I'm responsible for the whole night, so I try to pick my openers whenever possible. I've had a few really notable opening acts. Not notable like they're big stars now, but notable like notably bad. When you first start out, you don't always get to pick your opening act, and there are other times when the promoter tries to muscle someone onto the show who isn't good. Years ago I did a show at a crusty rock club in Philadelphia. The booker insisted I have this guy open for me. She said he was new to comedy but would "sell a lot of tickets." I'm not sure how many of the fifty people who showed up were there to see his *first-ever attempt at comedy*, but I do know he was booed off the stage. He didn't have any structured jokes and was just rambling, hoping something funny would come out. Getting booed off the stage is a pretty extreme occurrence in any situation. It's especially weird when the people booing are allegedly your friends and family.

The show in Durham was great, but there was a tiny moment of tension afterward because my check was calculated wrong. Getting paid after a show is always a bit nerve-racking. I usually get paid based on how many people show up, and in that situation you sort of have to trust that if they say two hundred people showed up, there weren't two hundred thirty people. There have also been situations where the person paying me is drunk, and I mean like "George Jones caught on dash cam during a DUI stop" drunk. I guess their attitude is "I work at a place that serves alcohol, so what's the problem?" Well, I've never been to a liquor store where the salespeople are drunk. And I don't want an intoxicated person figuring out my pay. But the promoter in Durham just made an innocent mistake that was fixed immediately. So since I'm an easygoing guy, as I may have already mentioned, we all headed to a nearby wine bar, where we were served by a waitress and bartender who weren't drunk.

I had the next day off, so I did a slow exit out of Durham. When I planned the trip, I couldn't decide whether to spend an extra night in Durham or Wilmington. For some reason, hotels in Durham were crazy expensive. I also thought it was a more interesting decision to spend the extra time in Wilmington. I had a coffee and some barbecue with Minori, and then spotted something sweet: a little announcement for my show written in bright pink chalk on the sidewalk.

Sidewalk announcement for my show. Durham, North Carolina.

I said good-bye to Minori, then went to my hotel, where I was meeting a local comic who would drive me to Wilmington and open for me there. His name was Mello Mike. I believe "Mello" is short for "mellow." I like when comedians go by some sort of nickname. My favorite example is Cedric the Entertainer.

Mello Mike lived up to his name. He was *totally* mellow and we made it to Wilmington without incident.

DEAD CROW
COMEDY ROOM

I first went to Wilmington, North Carolina, in 2010. I didn't know much about it, but I knew the venue I was playing, the Nutt Street Comedy Room, only held, like, a hundred people. In my mind I could sell that out easily. The default number of shows there was two, but I said, "Let's do three." Had I known how that would turn out, I would've said, "Let's do three. I want to look out and a see a bunch of empty chairs." When I made the bold decision to add that third one, I didn't take into account that it was Halloween weekend, when people want to be out on the streets acting like assholes and don't want to be cooped up in a club listening to a low-energy comic tell his amazing subtle jokes. There was also a little promotional glitch: they made a poster for the show that didn't list the showtimes. It just said my name, the name of the club, and the dates. I found myself at a table with some people, and one of them mentioned she'd made the poster. I said, "Oh, you left off the showtimes." I expected her to go, "Yeah, sorry about that." Instead she said, "Well I didn't think I needed to include that because people know who you are." What does that even mean? People know who I am? So you don't include showtimes? I know who U2 are, but if I saw a poster for their show, it would list showtimes. Did she think people would look at my poster and go, "Oh, Todd Barry is in town. You know what that means! Shows are Friday and Saturday at eight, with an added ten thirty show on Saturday because Todd thinks he's more popular than he actually is"?

I returned to Wilmington in 2015 to play the Dead Crow Comedy Room, booked and co-owned by a comic named Timmy Sherrill, who also booked and co-owned Nutt Street. This time I just scheduled two shows for Friday night.

I arrived on Thursday and started wandering. I walked by a little theater that had a production of Sam Shepard's *A Lie of the Mind*. I thought, *Hmmmm, seeing theater in Wilmington, North Carolina, sounds like an interesting prospect. But what if it's a tiny theater and there aren't a lot of people there? Will I feel self-conscious? Will the actors freak out because a big New York celeb is in the audience?* (I'm being playful, but also, I did think this.) I looked more closely at the poster for the show (it included the dates and showtimes) and found out there was no performance on Thursday. So I wandered around a bit. Got some wings at a place called the Copper Penny, then discovered another theater option. A play called *Clybourne Park* playing at a more traditional performing-arts hall. I mulled it over for a while. *Do I really want to sit through a play, or am I too antsy? What else would I do instead?* So I bought a ticket.

The first act of the play was set in a house recently sold by a white couple to a black family. The second act was set in the same house fifty years later, when that house was now in a predominantly black neigh-borhood. I didn't know what to expect, but it was compelling and well acted and I felt it was a bold choice. Like when I went to the basilica in Asheville.

Whenever a comic friend tweets that they're doing a show in Wilmington, they get a direct message from me: *Go to the snake museum. Trust me.* I discovered the Cape Fear Serpentarium on my first trip to Wilmington and it's one of my all-time favorite museum experiences. Tanks of gigantic, beautiful snakes and lizards—many of whom could kill you easily—all in a manageable not-overwhelming-sized building.

I headed back to my hotel via the riverwalk rather than the main street, not sure if I really wanted to do that or thought I should want to do that. *Todd, I noticed you took the riverwalk back instead of the main*

street. That just confirmed my hunch that you're an interesting dude with a healthy curiosity about life! And yes, I heard about the basilica in Asheville.

I usually get to venues at least ninety minutes early. Sometimes it's a good idea, like to make sure all the microphones and seats are set up, and also to beat the audience there to minimize preshow interaction. I did that this time, only to find the door locked. A couple of my crazed fans were also waiting, so it was awkward. You don't want your fans seeing you unable to get into your own show. I prefer them to think I'm airlifted from the Hilton to the helipad that's on the roof of most comedy clubs.

I went to a coffee shop and killed some time until the club opened. Things took a DRAMATIC TURN when Mello Mike arrived. I sell semifancy hand-printed posters after the show and had left them in Mello Mike's car. He was going to bring them to the show. Well, he either left them at his brother's house, where he was staying, or he took a different car to the show, but he didn't have my posters. This gave me something else to think about other than doing a good show. Selling merch on the road is a bit of a hassle when you tour at my level (I don't have roadies or a tour manager). So things like this can happen. But since the posters are marked up 900 percent, it's hard not to get upset. So Mello kept in touch with his brother, and I kept in touch with Mello about keeping in touch with his brother. I monitored the situation like I was waiting for an organ transplant. Mello assured me that his brother was on the way. Eventually he showed up, and, according to my records, I sold seven posters.

Both shows that night were sold out and much better than my previous trip to Wilmington, where I had to have two women thrown out because they wouldn't shut up. I had tried several times to let them know they were talking too loud, but it didn't work. I don't like getting people thrown out, and afterward I always feel like I got into a brawl, but sometimes there's no choice. I did a show at Caroline's in New York City years ago. There was a couple sitting at a front table talking to each other like they were on a date at a restaurant, except it was near a stage I was performing on. I asked them to be quiet and the woman said something like, "We don't have to be quiet."

"Well you kind of do."

"Uhhh, no we don't . . . ," she said as the perfectly timed shadow of a six-foot-five bouncer approached and proceeded to toss them.

After the late show at the Dead Crow I got roped into doing an interview with some dude who worked at the club who had a Web series. He seemed like a nice guy and I think he helped me sell merch, so I felt like I owed him. What I didn't realize was that the show was called *The Shit Show* and he did the whole thing in this super-awkward character where he didn't react to your questions in any sort of logical way. If it were my Web series I would've warned me about this. But maybe the comedic tension he wanted to create was more natural if he didn't warn me. But like I said, I owed the guy a favor. He helped me sell those seven posters.

MARCH 22, 2015—NEW BRUNSWICK, NEW JERSEY
THE STRESS FACTORY

I've been to the Stress Factory several times in the past eighteen years. It's a full-time comedy club that has some good things going for it: it's close to New York, it has a nice low stage that makes you feel connected to the audience, and there's no *check spot*. If you hang out with a comic more than twenty minutes, you'll hear them complain about the *check spot*. The *check spot* is a bizarre comedy club practice where the waiter or waitress gives the audience the bills for their food and drink in the middle of the show. So you can be onstage playing to a captive audience, then suddenly the waitstaff starts dropping the checks, and chaos ensues. Some audience members handle it well. They just put a credit card down while still keeping their eyes on the show. Other people, especially large groups, freak out and start dividing up the check. If you've ever seen a group of people in a restaurant laboring over a bill, imagine that going on at a table ten feet from where you're performing. Club owners rationalize the practice by saying it reduces the number of *walkouts*—people walking out on their checks. When I hear this excuse I always think, *A tiny percentage of the crowd* might *walk out on their checks, so you you're going to tarnish one hundred percent of the shows? How are you marketing your club? You really have that many dirtbags who walk out on their checks? Todd Barry fans don't walk out on their checks. Maybe you should start weeding out your e-mail list.* Also, how come they don't have a "check spot" when you go to a restaurant?

But the Stress Factory doesn't have a check spot. At the end of the show, they give you a little ticket to show you paid, which you then show to a door person before you exit.

The lack of a check spot is good thing, but there's one thing about the Stress Factory that I haven't loved in the past: the way they start the show. They play a video of upcoming comics, which is fine, but they also play these "animals gone crazy" videos, including one where a cat bites a guy on the inner thigh. But that's nothing compared to what happens next. There's a phone attached to the wall onstage and the host of the show, often the owner, comedian Vinnie Brand, makes a prank call based on an audience suggestion. I remember one time where a guy in the audience suggested calling his grandmother, who'd hit a deer with her car recently. So Vinnie, or whoever was hosting, called up the grandmother and told her the deer died. The old woman had the human reaction of being upset by this. I stood in the wings mortified.

I remember telling someone at the club that I didn't like the prank-call opening. They said, "But it really gets the audience going." Yes, it does. So would shooting audience members with a paintball gun. Or strippers. There are a lot of things I could think of that would get the audience going but not set the best tone.

I returned to the Stress Factory in 2015 for a Sunday night show. There's usually a hotel offered when you play there, but I don't usually take it because it's easy enough to get a ride or take a train home from there. This time I did take the hotel because I wanted to check out the city. I got there that afternoon and started roaming. Sat at the bar of a place called Tumulty's for lunch, a few feet away from a guy in a suit and sunglasses drinking a martini, bantering with some women sitting a few seats down. He was one of those characters who make me instantly curious and wish I had the guts to talk to them: *"Sorry to bother you, but I couldn't help noticing you're drinking a martini during the day and also wearing sunglasses inside."*

"I've been coming to this place for twenty years. They make a great martini and I have sensitive eyes."

"My name is Todd, but you probably knew that because I'm famous."

"I don't know who you are. I'm Roger."

"Well, fair enough on the sunglasses, Roger, but how are you able to drink a martini during the day? It looks like you're dressed for work."

"I have a one-man law practice. I can handle one martini at lunch."

"One-man law firm? I'm kind of a one-man band myself. No second martini?"

Roger would smile and raise his glass. "As far as you're concerned."

I walked around a bit more and had a panicked feeling that I shouldn't have taken the hotel, like I was going to go nuts staying here even for just one night. But I still had the option of leaving that night.

Doing just one show on a Sunday night instead of five over a weekend was a good idea. I got a nice group of actual fans. Also, there was no prank call at the beginning (I don't know if they stopped doing it, or maybe the onstage *prank phone* was out of order).

I had decided not to stay overnight at the hotel but still wanted to go out in New Brunswick before heading home. I'd gotten a ride with the opening act, Dan Shaki. Dan is one of those guys who looks like he's in a bad mood, but then you talk to him and he's perfectly pleasant. Not *perky* like me, but still good company. When Dan isn't doing comedy, he runs a walking-tour business. I ran into him once on the street midtour. No, I didn't draw attention to myself.

I wasn't sure my girlfriend, who had taken a train to meet me, would be into going out, but she was. So she, Dan, and I found a place called Clydz. It was perfect. It was quiet; they were serving food. And it provided my best memory of the night. As the waiter was putting down a place mat and silverware in front of me, he said, "I'm gonna set you up for success."

MARCH 27, 2015—ANNAPOLIS, MARYLAND
RAMS HEAD LIVE

Dan Shaki and I got to Annapolis the day of our show, the day after my birthday (just putting that out there for next year).

I checked into my hotel and encountered one of my biggest (and pettiest) travel pet peeves: the hotel room with something *slightly* wrong with it. Half the hotels I check into have something slightly broken, something I can't figure out. If it's like a toilet that doesn't flush, then it's obvious you have to call for help. But when something is just a little bit out of order, you spend time deciding whether to do something about it or just deal with it for the fourteen hours you'll be at the hotel. In Annapolis, I started to open up my shades and discovered I had a view of Annapolis National Cemetery. But the shades didn't go up all the way; they were locked with some sort of stopper. I tried and tried to open them up all the way. I took deep breaths and gave myself the usual pep talk: *You're a smart guy, Todd. VERY smart. WOW, you're smart. I bet you're even smart enough to open hotel shades. You don't need to call down to the front desk for help. People dumber than you probably open shades every day.*

I tried some more and couldn't get it open. So I called down to the front desk, and they said the line that puts me into a gentle, internal rage: "We'll send up an *engineer* to look at it." An *engineer*? Hotels love sending up an engineer. On several occasions I've called the front desk because the TV remote wasn't working. Same reply: "We'll send up an engineer." For a broken remote? Can't you just talk me through it over the phone? No, they can't, so they must send up an engineer to give you new AA batteries. In this case the engineer showed up and there *was* something wrong with the shades. It took long enough to fix it, but I felt vindicated.

The show was at a place called Rams Head Live. My friend Tom Papa said he had a good show there, so I looked into it and got booked.

It's a very professionally run seated venue that usually books seasoned musical acts like Leon Russell and Los Lobos. I did a quick sound check. It's not like my show is Cirque du Soleil or anything, but you'd be surprised how people can screw up a show that just involves setting up a microphone and some lights. I did a show years ago in Dallas with Louis C.K. I went on to do my opening set, and my mic didn't work. I waited a bit, and it still didn't work. So I made the bold (and correct) choice to step away from the mic, put on my best Broadway projected voice, and tell the audience, "I'll be back." I walked offstage, they fixed the problem, and I went back out and had a pretty good show; the audience understood what was going on. The thing that amused me about the incident was that there were two shows that night. The early one was Louis and me. The late show was headlined by a band called the Polyphonic Spree. If you're not familiar with them, they're a band with about three million members. So the same people who'd just sound-checked a huge band with a chorus couldn't have one mic set up for an opening act who just talks?

But there were no technical problems at Rams Head. It was quite full and the people were responsive. The only problem was a table of awful people who yelled out that one of them was celebrating a birth-day. Part of the reason I try to do one-night shows at non-comedy venues is to avoid situations like this. I was a bit surprised it happened here. One of my most satisfying memories as a comic was when I was onstage at club called Stand Up NY. I turned to my left and a woman was HOLDING UP A SIGN that said, "HER BIRTHDAY!" with an arrow pointing to the friend sitting next to her. The woman holding the sign had a look on her face that said, "I bet you're as excited about this as I am!" I looked at the sign, then turned away and finished my set without mentioning it. You might be saying, *But, Todd, birthdays are exciting. You mentioned yours in the first sentence of this chapter.* Yes, but I didn't yell it out in the middle of your show. Also, there's a big difference in my birthday and everyone else's.

I had some good moments talking to the crowd. One *showstopping* moment was when I asked a guy in the audience how much a house in Annapolis costs.

"Depends," he deadpanned.

It's always great when an audience member makes me laugh.

"Yeah, I guess it *would* depend. There's really no other way to answer that. Probably a stupid question!"

I talked to a family at the front table. One of the kids had seen me a few days ago in New Brunswick (I guess he was visiting there) and decided to bring his family, including his father, who was clearly not into me. This kind of thing happens quite a bit. A kid drags his parents to my show and they're not into it, or a guy brings his girlfriend, but she hates me.

After the show the son had me add a second autograph to the poster he'd bought in New Brunswick and mentioned he was going to see me a third time at my upcoming show in Arlington, Virginia. I hate when people see me multiple shows of mine in such a short span of time. I realize it's flattering, but comedy is about surprise, and although there are spontaneous moments in every performance, if you see me three times in a week, you're pretty much seeing the same show. I can't imagine the third show having the same impact as the first one. The exception would be if I'm doing one of my crowd-work shows, which are all banter with the audience. But he was a nice kid, and I guess it's one of those "good problems to have."

Another guy approached me holding one of those disposable cameras you used to buy at Walgreens until you got a better phone. I'm fine with taking pictures, but this guy didn't want to be in the shot. This happens occasionally. I told him he had to be in the picture, too. I'm not going to pose for you like we're doing a shoot for the *ripped abs* edition of *Men's Health*.

On our way out of Annapolis the next day, I spotted something beautiful: a sign for "Carlson's Donuts & Thai Kitchen." I told Dan we were eating there. I may have asked if he wanted to eat there, but I probably just told him.

I loved our waitress. She took our order while wiping down the adjacent table. A hoity-toity person would've been upset by this kind of multitasking, but not me. I found it charming.

GALLERY5

I drove to Richmond with Dan Shaki the day before the show. This was my second trip to Richmond and also my second time performing at Gallery5, a cool little space that seats one hundred or so. Checked into the Richmond Marriott, whose attached sports bar/restaurant boasts the "biggest TV in Richmond." I stole a glance at it. *Extremely* large television set!

Dan was staying at a different hotel a few miles away because I paid for his room with some reward points. I didn't put him in a different hotel to *show him who's* boss. We had the whole night free, so I thought we'd head over to Gallery5 to see what was going on. Maybe they had a good show that we could see for FREE, since I was doing a show there the following night. There was some sort of burlesque party happening that sounded intriguing. I've done comedy in a few burlesque shows and they can be fun to watch, mainly because each act is only on for about three minutes. I'm a fan of things that don't last long.

I walked up to the woman at the door and said, "Hi, I'm performing here tomorrow night, just wanted to see if we could see the show." Nothing. She had no idea what I was talking about. I didn't want to say, "Hey, it's a standard showbiz courtesy to let someone into a show if they're doing their own show there the next night." At some point I realized the woman didn't work for the venue or the promoter who brought me to town. She worked with the burlesque group, so there was no reason she should know about my show or let me in for free. I stood there a minute deciding whether I wanted to pay, but it seemed like more of a private-party vibe as much as a show, and I thought we'd feel out of place.

We headed to a restaurant called Saison, which had a great adult-hipster (as opposed to PBR hipster) gastropub vibe. We sat at the bar. I think I ordered wine, but resisted ordering carrot cake with "black pepper cream cheese ice cream and curried carrots." I'd asked the bartender if the carrot cake was "gigantic." As far as dumb questions go, I thought this was a good one. He said no, but it could be shared. I knew Dan Shaki, but we weren't to the point where we'd share a dessert. (I wouldn't even let him stay in the same hotel as me.)

After the hipster bar we went to a place called GWARbar, named for and owned by members of the Richmond band Gwar, who describe themselves as "Earth's only openly extraterrestrial rock band." They perform in elaborate costumes and spray fake blood at the crowd. I saw them when we were both booked at the same festival in Austin. They were really good musicians and their show was nuts, but as a performer, all I could think was, *You go through all the trouble to tour, and you perform anonymously? Like, you're public and anonymous at the same time? Don't you want/need people coming up to you after the show and saying, "Great job!"*? I felt so needy.

I was surprised that GWARbar wasn't full of people who looked like they were in Gwar. It was a nice mix of people young and old, cool and uncool—seemed like it was a neighborhood bar that had been there fifty years. We left before getting a drink because it was too loud. Yes, the bar named for a rock band played loud rock music.

The next day we pursued a *hot tip* from a friend to take a drive on Monument Avenue to look at "pretty houses and statues." Sounded good to me, so Dan picked me up. The houses were pretty. So pretty that when I got back to the hotel, I put "Richmond real estate" into Google. I found beautiful houses on Monument Avenue ten times the size of my apartment that I could afford. I wish I wanted to move to Richmond. But I had said the same thing when I went to Asheville. Maybe I can get a place in both cities. That would be a great topic for a talk show appearance. *"So, Todd, you live in New York, right? Or did you move to LA?"*

"Neither, Jimmy Fallon. I actually have homes in Richmond and Asheville."

"Really? You don't even keep a crash pad in New York?"

"No, Jimmy. I took the money I spent on rent and use it to pay off two mortgages."

"Wow. Two mortgages."

"Yes, Jimmy, and both houses are mansions."

"Wow again. How do you get to your gigs?"

"Well, Jimmy, I'll tell you. [lowers voice] But it's got to be a secret."

Jimmy leans in. Todd whispers loudly, "Both cities have airports."

The crowd goes nuts over this incredible zing.

I was a little worried about ticket sales for Richmond because Hannibal Buress was in town the same night playing a theater. Hannibal is one of those guys I knew when he'd just moved to New York but went on to zoom past me career-wise. But both of our shows sold out.

Before my show I spotted a guy who seemed like potential trouble. He was just a little *louder* than he needed to be and seemed like he'd be capable of *outbursts*. I usually have a good eye for this kind of thing and he did turn out to be jerk. He interrupted a few times and was eventually thrown out. On his way to the exit he yelled some sort of "you suck"–themed comment. I like when this happens because it says to the audience, "Here's why they're throwing me out." Hannibal was having an after-party at some club where he and another guy were DJing. I like when I cross paths with friends on the road, but Hannibal had a bunch of well-wishers, so we didn't talk long. It wasn't like a postshow meet-up at Denny's, where you spend the time shit-talking comedy club bookers and comedians you hate. Although our time was brief, I probably made sure I made him feel bad about playing to seventeen hundred more people than I did that night, even though I've been doing comedy longer. I hope I did this. Not giving him shit for doing a bigger show than mine would be a real missed opportunity.

It was fun to see Hannibal, but I left his party early. Too loud!

THE THIRSTY HIPPO

I first performed in Hattiesburg in 2013. It was my first-ever show in Mississippi, so I was excited to check it off the list. The show started off good, but then I heard a dude talking loudly on the side of the stage, which is bad enough, but he was also talking to my girlfriend. I gently mentioned that he was talking too loud and asked if he could maybe keep it down. He responded in a shitty "I'm not sorry" way rather than a "I'm sorry I was distracting you by hitting on your girlfriend ten feet from the stage" way. He seemed like a sad, lonely drunk, and he eventually moved on to someone else. After the show I found out he was a cop. I started imagining scenarios where I handled the interruption differently.

"Hey, *asshole*, I need two things from you or I won't be able to continue with this *amazing* show: Number one, shut the fuck up. Number two, stop talking to my girl."

The guy would keep talking.

Then I'd put it out to the crowd: "This guy needs to shut the fuck up and show us some respect. Am I right?"

No one responds because they all know he's a cop.

"Did you not hear me, motherfucker?" I'd say.

The guy would laugh in the way you'd laugh if you were a cop and the comedian cursing at you was the only person in the room who didn't know.

"Well," I'd say, "I've never done this before . . ."

I'd jump into the crowd and tackle the guy. He'd quickly subdue me and put me in cuffs, making my worst nightmare (going to prison) come true. It would all be worth it because I'd become a legend among comics, and at least one indie rock band would write a song about me.

I landed in Biloxi a day before the 2015 show and drove about ninety minutes to my hotel with Jamie Arrington, a comic who'd also booked me the last time I was in town. Hattiesburg is not the best roaming-around city, although I did walk into a nearby CVS. A guy approached me who said he was the doorman for my show that night. Not sure that counts as getting recognized.

Leatha's BBQ. Hattiesburg, Mississippi.

I wanted some real Southern food, so Jamie brought me to a barbecue place called Leatha's. I fancy myself a guy who loves barbecue, but I'm not a lunatic about it. I won't debate South Carolina mustard-based sauce vs. Kansas City sauce sweetened with molasses. Plus I almost always order chicken at barbecue places. I'm not sure if you're supposed to order chicken at a barbecue place. I mean, you're allowed to, but I feel like the real macho barbecue guys go for beef or pork. I once ate at a barbecue place in Austin and decided to mix things up by ordering brisket. The guy serving it asked, "Lean or fatty?" Really? That's a choice? People really want fatty beef by choice? I pull the fat off bacon. It's true. Eat bacon with me sometime if you don't believe me.

The people who worked at Leatha's were lovely. One especially lovely moment: I was sipping on a bottle of Diet Coke when a nice older man, probably the owner, walked over and put another bottle on the table next to the one I was drinking. I've had bartenders refill my glass when I'm drinking Diet Coke at a bar, but this guy gave me a whole new bottle. It was a Diet Coke refill scenario unlike any one I've ever experienced!

At some point in the trip the subject of the KKK came up, and I asked Jamie if he'd ever seen them. He said, "I've lived in Mississippi and Illinois, and the only time I saw the KKK was in Illinois." Later he told me it was a sad little "attempt at a rally" by a small group of Klansmen in the Chicago suburbs. I tell that to people whenever they trash the South.

The show that night was much better than the first one. I had a good opening act, a New Orleans comic named Andrew Polk, who had e-mailed when he heard I was doing a run of Southern shows and wanted to see if I needed an opener. Andrew has the three qualities you want in an opening act: 1) He's funny. 2) He's not annoying. 3) He has a car. I put "funny" as my number one requirement, but I should probably switch that with "not annoying." And of course a not-annoying and unfunny comic with a car will do in a pinch.

The venue was a place called the Thirsty Hippo, which had a nice low stage and the added feature of no one hitting on my girlfriend inches from me. To be fair, she wasn't with me on this trip, but there was no one that rude in the crowd. I had another minor problem with a photographer from a local paper who'd asked in advance if she could take pictures. For some reason she used a flash (even though she was standing in the back of the room, and there were already spotlights aimed at the stage, and I've never experienced a real photographer using a flash during a show). I said some very gentle "I wish you weren't doing that" types of things, then the flashing stopped. I found out later that she left and the pictures were never posted anywhere.

I told the audience I was going to Birmingham the next day and a guy in the crowd said that wasn't a fun city. I asked how he knew that. He said, "You know, from all the documentaries."

Documentaries? Really? You've seen more than one documentary about the fun potential in Birmingham, Alabama? Like, you saw one documentary on this subject and you wanted a second opinion? Luckily you have the Netflix membership that includes DVDs!

Next stop, Birmingham, Alabama. The city from the documentaries.

IRON CITY

I drove to Birmingham with Andrew. We stopped at a great barbecue place in Tuscaloosa called Dreamland. The food was great, and now I get to say I ate lunch in Tuscaloosa.

The last time I had been in Birmingham was 2007. I played a cool place called the Bottletree Cafe. I was looking for an opening act, and the club booker was going over some options with me. He mentioned a few bands and a comedian, then said, "We also have an eleven-year-old folksinger—"

Stop right there.

The idea of an eleven-year-old opening for me sounded hilarious, but before I committed to this I had one question for the booker: "I just need to know that he's into doing this. Like, he really likes playing and it's not a stage-mother type thing?" I was assured that this kid was the real deal. I've been to casting offices in New York when there's an audition going on involving kids, and you see these awful parents bringing in hair-sprayed little boys and girls, and you can just see the ugly urgency in the parents' eyes, and I didn't want any part of that type of thing.

The kid's name was Walker Yancey. A friend described him as an "avant-garde Woody Guthrie" and that was pretty accurate.

Iron City. Birmingham, Alabama.

I talked to him a little bit backstage. Normally I don't like precocious kids, but he was organically precocious—an actual smart kid who shared Bob Dylan quotes.

I played a much bigger place in 2015 called Iron City. Marilyn Manson was playing there a few weeks after me. I was surprised Marilyn and I were playing the same-sized venue, and I'm guessing he'd wonder about the same thing. I could imagine him on the phone with his agent: "I'm playing the same places as Todd *fucking* Barry? The *comedian*? The really great comedian? I mean, he's super talented—I could never do what he does—but I'm a rock star. Is that what it's come to?" His agent would reply, "But Todd's doing a fully seated show, which significantly reduces the capacity." There would be a pause, then, "If I ever see Todd Barry on the upcoming events list of any venue I'm booked at, you're fired!"

The stage manager at Iron City said they were required to buy all-black furniture for Marilyn's dressing room. I asked, "Why can't you just buy slipcovers?" If you're into sports metaphors, my question would be considered a "home run."

About a hundred fifty people showed up that night. It was a big venue with a high stage, but it felt great. If I want to play the same venues as Marilyn Manson, I have to get used to high stages. I mean, when I inevitably become an *arena comic*, the stages are going to be *really* high. After the show I went to a bar called Parkside that had the pleasant surprise of an Asian-fusion food truck in their back patio.

The next day Andrew and I got some coffee at a place called Revelator, one of those serious coffee shops that have maybe five things on the menu. A customer there asked me for a photo, said he was sorry he'd missed the show. He seemed like a nice guy, and I don't remember his excuse for not going, but c'mon, how many chances are you gonna get to see Todd Barry in Birmingham, Alabama?

I'm sure I'll be back, but next time I'll have this in my contract:

"Mr. Barry requires crimson couches and easy chairs in his dressing room. You may accomplish this with slipcovers. No need to buy new furniture."

40 WATT CLUB

I love touring the South, but I have to admit I had an ulterior motive for the 2015 run of Southern dates: I got invited to a wedding in Athens, Georgia. Actually I think I invited myself to a wedding in Athens, Georgia.

The guy getting married was a comedy writer named Jon Schroeder. People call him Tall Jon because he's six foot ten. I worked with Jon when I was writing for *The Sarah Silverman Program* and when I did voices for the animated show *Bob's Burgers*, which he writes on. Like most of my friends, he had his wedding in an inconvenient location, but just close enough to a convenient location that you notice and get angry. He did, however, have the single best thing I've ever read on a wedding invitation:

Shuttles will be available for guests who want to leave early.

That's a half a step away from saying, "We know you don't want to come to our wedding."

Attending Jon's wedding involved flying to Atlanta (where he should've had it) and then driving to Athens, about ninety minutes away.

I've performed in Athens a few times, so I thought, why not *bankroll* my trip to the wedding by booking a tour around it? So I got an Athens show the day before at the legendary 40 Watt Club, then added the dates in Hattiesburg and Birmingham.

Andrew Polk and I drove to town the day of the show. On the way there we listened to the Kim Gordon episode of Marc Maron's *WTF* podcast. We stopped at a Carl's Jr., but the line of construction workers was so long we went across the street to the less *happening* McDonald's.

There was a little day-before-the-wedding get-together a few blocks from the club. The problem was it was an outdoor event, there were gray skies, and I'm terrified of lightning. Truly terrified. If you're walking with me and I see lightning, I *will* run away from you. I've done this before. I was on Pete Holmes's podcast and he asked, "Why are you afraid of lightning?"

"Because it's electricity that's coming from the sky," I answered. This was a live podcast, and my lightning line received *thunderous* laughter.

I didn't actually see any lightning at this party, but the gray skies meant there was the *potential* for lightning, so that was enough reason to run back to the club. On my way out I let people know they could get into my show if they just said they were part of the wedding, a kind and totally unnecessary gesture on my part.

I got to the club too early and it was locked, and I felt panicked that I might be stuck outside in a thunderstorm. Eventually someone showed up and I got in. Later on the woman who books the club, Velena Vego, arrived with her husband, David Lowery, from the bands Camper Van Beethoven and Cracker. I'd put the word out to Doug Benson and Sarah Silverman, who were also attending the wedding, that they could do guest spots on my show if they wanted. There were a lot of other comics attending the wedding, but I didn't want the possibility of six people on before me. This was my fifth time playing the 40 Watt, and it was the best show yet. Sarah and Doug didn't end up doing sets, but it was my biggest crowd, and I felt loose.

After the show I noticed Doug Benson in the back, and he ended up helping me sell my posters. I was told Jon Hamm from *Mad Men* was also there but left right after it ended. I know Jon a little because we have mutual friends, so I assume he bolted to avoid being mobbed and not because my show wasn't amazing.

After the poster sales were done, a bunch of us walked over to the prewedding party until that ended, then went on a search for a nearby karaoke bar (meaning other people wanted to go to a karaoke bar, and I followed). We finally found it, and much to my delight it was closed.

On the wedding shuttle. Somewhere in Georgia.

I went to the wedding the next day. Shuttle buses stopped at each of the hotels to take us to a farm where the ceremony and reception were happening. One of the buses got lost and pulled over on the freeway waiting for another one to catch up. The second bus went the wrong way down a one-way street.

At one point during the ceremony I experienced the single greatest moment of any wedding I've ever attended. Most of the guests had taken their seats in this beautiful outdoor setting, when about a hundred yards away, a man slowly approached. I guess it was the Bob Marley T-shirt that made him stand out. I've always been a fan of the underdressed guy at the wedding or funeral, but this guy took it to a new level. I thought it was a comedy bit set up by Jon, and I bet he wished that as well.

I'd asked Tall Jon to put me at the *celeb table* at the reception, so he sat me with Jon Hamm, Sarah Silverman, and Michael Sheen. *Todd, that's quite a group of VIPs! I would kill to know what you guys talked about—to be a "fly on the wall" for that conversation. And yes, Todd, I know you guys were eating outside. You know what I mean, Todd. Serve us some hot "VIP table at a Georgia wedding" gossip.*

I'd love to, but the only thing I remember is Jon Hamm saying he was getting up to get more food from the buffet. *That's it, Todd?!*

Yeah. That's it. I have a weird arbitrary memory. I can remember the name of someone I met once twelve years ago but forget the name of someone I've met six times in the past three months. Same with remembering movies. I'll say something like, "You have to see *City of God*. It's fantastic." But I couldn't tell you one frame of what happened in that movie. So, it's the same with conversations. I've got no hot gossip to report.

Like most comedian weddings, it was relaxed and really fun. I didn't even need to take advantage of the "You can bolt early, we'll even provide transportation" clause.

ONE LONGFELLOW SQUARE

Something unprecedented occurred the last time I played Portland, Maine: I was overpaid. *Todd, what are you talking about? I've seen you onstage. There's no amount of money that's too much for sharing your genius.* Wow, thanks. But I really was overpaid. I don't mean the guy accidentally added a "0" and paid me $500,000 when my contract said $50,000. (Oops, I just revealed how much I get per show. Hee hee!) I mean I was guaranteed a large amount of cash, but there was not a large amount of people in the audience. It was pretty dismal.

For some reason they had me doing two shows at a pretty massive venue, and I probably played to about forty people the whole weekend. I remember waiting to get paid after the second show; I was prepared for some sort of "Todd, we really took a hit on this one. Can you give us a break?" conversation, but it didn't happen. The booker graciously handed me a stack of cash, which included a few hundred bucks for travel money (plus he paid for my hotel). I remember afterward thinking I should've given them a little rebate, but there are were several reasons I didn't:

1. I preferred to walk away with the amount of money I was paid, rather than that amount minus a rebate.
2. No booker had ever given me a surprise bonus when more people showed up than expected, so why would I give them a rebate when the crowd was tiny?
3. I wasn't sure the guy paying me was the guy who was losing money. Maybe he was the guy handing the money off to me, and if I gave him a rebate he would pocket that and tell his boss he'd paid me in full.

I kind of liked reason three, because it implied I was interested in justice, but really, I just wanted the money. The guy who paid me seemed like a straight-up dude, and I doubt he would've skimmed anything.

I arrived in Portland a day before the 2015 show, ready to fulfill a promise I'd made to myself since my last visit that involved tea and my feet. On my previous trip I'd walked by a place called Soak, a combination foot spa/tearoom. They had a menu with various treatments and tea combinations. You just sat there, they did some shit to your feet, and you sipped tea. I remember looking at their menu the last time, thinking, *I should do this*, but not following through. Maybe I had a premonition that I was about to get overpaid and I didn't deserve it.

I looked up Soak and found a place called Soakology. I assumed it was the same place and that I'd remembered the name wrong. I headed in that direction, stopping off at a food court/market–type place for a bowl of really good corn chowder. On my way out of the market a dude running a cupcake booth recognized me and offered me a free cupcake. I'm a bit inconsistent when it comes to healthy eating. I'll say no to a cupcake in the afternoon but eat a plate of chicken fingers and fries after a show. And maybe some chips before while I'm waiting for the chicken fingers to arrive. Somehow I had the willpower to decline the offer. I was pretty proud of myself. I like cupcakes and I like free stuff. This was a wonderful combination of both, and I said no.

I made my way over to Soakology. I didn't have an appointment. I was banking on a Portland, Maine, foot spa/tearoom having availability on a Wednesday. My hunch was correct and they were able to take me right away. I looked at the menu of options and chose the "refreshing aromatherapy" treatment.

I went downstairs and put on some slippers. The tea was good, and, at first, the treatment relaxing. That changed when the woman pulled out a pumice-type thing designed to scrape feet. She rubbed a little too hard on my heel and ripped open some skin, causing the *refreshing* aromatherapy to become less *refreshing*. She was very apologetic, and I was very forgiving. I mean, sometimes I flub a word when I'm doing a show (and end up *injuring* the audience). Also, she'd mentioned she'd seen me on *Flight of the Conchords*, so maybe she was nervous, like how I'd be if I were giving a pedicure to the Beatles.

The next day I took a ferry to a place called Peaks Island, which I'd heard was very "quiet." I got there and "quiet" is not the word. If I did a show for an audience made up entirely of ninety-year-olds who only spoke Portuguese, I wouldn't have experienced this much silence. I poked around a little, bought something to drink at the super-quiet market, and walked past the Umbrella Cover Museum, which really is an umbrella cover museum. Unfortunately it's only open during the summer, or I would have absolutely gone in. (Try not to think of the three or four great sentences I would've written about the museum had they been open.)

Popcorn shop. Portland, Maine.

I found a magazine that had a big article that described Peaks Island as a place where "people still drop by unannounced." If I were looking for a house and the real estate agent said, "This is a place where people still drop by unannounced," I would say, "Thanks for the warning. Do you have an island where people call first?" If someone drops by unannounced in New York, it's to tell me my music is too loud. Or, in the case of an insane upstairs neighbor I had many years ago, to tell me she was hearing too much noise, even though I was brushing my teeth at the time and my roommate was in his room reading.

The Portland show was the first of three New England shows. My opening act for this run was a Boston comic named Ken Reid, who had opened for me on a previous tour of the area and, besides being funny, was really easy to work with and up for anything. (For me "up for anything" means maybe getting some food after 1:00 a.m.)

I arrived at the venue to find that the dressing room was a mess and there was nothing from my hospitality rider out (the *rider* is where you list your backstage food and drink demands). It was like they didn't know there was going to be a show that night. I'm not a *diva*, but if I show up and see an overflowing garbage can, a Mr. Coffee that has a half a pot that's clearly been there for a week, and worst of all, the requisite toilet that hasn't been cleaned in ages, I get upset. Yes, I know I mentioned a dirty toilet at the Toledo venue, and I didn't seem upset. Good eye. I think the Toledo toilet may have been *hilariously* dirty, whereas this one was just disgusting. Or maybe I was in a better mood, or I was distracted by the broken door. But I'm pretty sure this one was more disgusting. In these situations, I don't yell and scream, but I will say something. I said something here, and someone came in and cleaned up a bit. Everyone was apologetic, so I didn't throw one of my Elton John–style temper tantrums.

The show was much better than my previous trip to Portland. It was packed. I made less money than last time I'd been there, but at least I didn't feel guilty when I got paid.

I wanted to go out after. Ken Reid mentioned that there was a bar in town that specialized in nonalcoholic cocktails. I don't drink a lot, but Ken doesn't drink at all (and has never, in fact, even tried alcohol, another reason he's easy to tour with). It sounded like a great idea, so we headed over to Vena's Fizz House and ordered a round of *mocktails*. I ordered a drink called the Kickstarter, made with ghost pepper and apple cider drinking vinegar. It was really delicious but also really intense, not the type of drink you guzzle before saying, "Hey, barkeep, hit me with another."

Ken and I stumbled out of the soda bar and headed to a place called Boda. I really love stylish Thai food. We didn't go there just so I could say, "We drank soda, then went to Boda."

APRIL 18, 2015—PAWTUCKET, RHODE ISLAND

THE MET

Before my Pawtucket show, my last Rhode Island show had been in 2009 at a place called Jerky's Live Music Hall, located on the second floor of a downtown Providence building. *Todd, you played a place called Jerky's. I bet that went well.* I don't mind doing a show at a place called Jerky's located on the second floor of a building, unless the first floor is occupied by a punk club called Club Hell that has a show going on at the same time as mine. I was booked upstairs, while an extremely loud punk band performed downstairs—with only a poorly soundproofed ceiling/floor between us. Sometimes during a show you're faced with obstacles that the audience isn't aware of, so you don't get sympathy from them. An example would be a chatty table up front. They might be so distracting you have to stop the show, but the people in the back of the club don't hear them, so you're banking on their figuring out there's a legitimate problem. This wasn't an issue at Jerky's that night. As they struggled to hear my punch lines, the audience was *very* aware of what I was up against. I made jokes about it and the show became about the other show. I felt the warm feeling of "Wow, this must suck for you, Todd, but you do your thing. We're with you."

I returned to Providence in 2015 the night after doing a show in Boston. Ken Reid dropped me at my hotel. There was a drag ball in town, and a lot of the ladies were staying at the hotel. They were in a festive mode, and that didn't end in the lobby. My room was near a particularly rambunctious group of them, so I stormed downstairs to get a new room. Once I had done that, I was glad the drag queens were there. I didn't really talk to any of them, but they were a refreshing change from the usual high school volleyball team or pharmaceutical salesperson conference that I usually find at the hotels I stay at.

After checking in, I went for a walk, not knowing at the time that I was about to become a hero. I went to a coffee shop. At one of the tables I spotted an iPad Mini next to an empty espresso cup. *Hmmmm. That seems like a weird way to save your seat while you go to the restroom.* So I grabbed the iPad and walked it over to the counter. "I found this on a table." The woman at the counter was very appreciative and even thanked me for not stealing it. Within a minute the coffee shop's phone rang. The person who answered said, "Did anyone turn in an iPad?" Yes, *someone* did. Not just anyone. Me. Half the reason I'm writing this book is to get the "I turned in someone's iPad" story to the wider audience it deserves.

Ken returned from Boston and drove me to the venue, which was actually in Pawtucket, Rhode Island, located in a building that was also home to a duckpin bowling alley (with a real person resetting the pins) as well as the Rhode Island Music Hall of Fame, which was not huge but pretty good for a small state.

The audience enjoyed when I pronounced their city as "PAW-tuckit" instead of the correct "Puh-TUCK-et." The best gift you can give an audience is your own stupidity. It was an easy laugh, so I milked it for ten minutes. (FULL DISCLOSURE: It was probably one minute.) You don't even have to be clever in these instances. Just keep saying something wrong in different sentences. "You have good restaurants here in *PAW-tuckit*." BWAHAHAHAHA. HUGE LAUGH. "Seriously, I might buy a house here in *PAW-tuckit*." GENIUS!

I went looking with Ken for some postshow food and found a steak house bar near the hotel. I like a good steak house bar. Usually quiet. I feel a bit out of my element, but in a good way. I had a glass of wine and some appetizers. I don't remember what we talked about. Probably how I found someone's iPad at a coffee shop and turned it in, and how cool it was that I did that.

THE BALLROOM
AT THE OUTER SPACE

Hamden, Connecticut, is near New Haven, the last Connecticut city I'd played, also with this promoter. My contract says I need to do seated shows (even in music venues where the audiences generally stand). I remember showing up for the New Haven gig and seeing maybe ten bar stools, which to them made it a seated show. They had also made a rather nice silkscreened poster, but there was nothing outside the club advertising my show. So if you'd walked by, you'd have had no idea anything was going on that night; it just looked like a bar. I asked if they'd thought of putting one of the posters outside, you know, to help serve the function of a poster. The guy acted like I was a marketing genius. "I didn't think of that," he responded.

I chatted with the owner, who seemed to really want the show to go well. I told him I was concerned that this wasn't the typical show they did there, and with most of the audience standing, there might be a lot of people talking. He ended up introducing the show and gave the audience a nice explanation of what to expect and how to behave. The stage was tiny and right next to the front door. Everyone who entered late was right next to me. Like so close, I could give everyone a neck rub as they walked in. I had been contacted by a guy I knew a little from Florida who now lived in the area and wanted to be on the guest list. He showed up late and was standing maybe a foot from me while I was performing. Of course, they couldn't find his name on the list, so he turned to me midjoke and gave me a "Can you help me out?" look. Sure, what else do I have going on? So I said, "He's good," and continued my show.

I booked a hotel in New Haven for the Hamden show but wasn't sure I wanted to stay over. Ken and I went to a famous pizza place called Frank Pepe. We were standing in a rather large line. I had noticed there was another Frank Pepe location right next door. I walked over there and the waitress said, "There's no wait here, and it's the same kitchen!" That's all I needed to hear.

After pizza Ken dropped me at my hotel and went to a record store. He had declined my insincere offer of a hotel room since he could just drive back to Boston after the show.

I got a little lost driving to the Hamden venue. It was in a weird strip mall/industrial park complex.

Once inside I realized I'd arrived at the second stop of my 2015 "make the promoter clean the greenroom" tour. The greenroom was filthy, especially the bathroom. Felt a little guilty watching the guy who booked me there clean the toilet, but he seemed to know it was a reasonable request.

I try to introduce my opening acts from an offstage microphone. I do this because I don't want to pass off that responsibility to someone who doesn't know how to do an intro, which is always a possibility. The biggest mistake people make with intros is not saying the comic's name at the end. So instead of "Our next comic is amazing. He's also a prolific author. Please welcome Todd Barry!" (*big applause*) they say, "Our next comic is Todd Barry. He's written a book. Um . . . okay. Here he is" (*confused smattering of applause*). Putting the name at the end propels the show. Another kind of bad intro often happens at college gigs. It's the *inappropriate information* intro. Someone with bad public-speaking skills goes up to the mic and mumbles something like, "Um, I want to tell you about the upcoming AIDS walk we are having. AIDS is a horrible epidemic that kills thousands of people every year. [*short pause*] Todd Barry is our comedian tonight. He's been on Comedy Central. Um, here he is."

Another reason I try to do the opening comic's intro is to let people know, "Hey, before I come out there, there's someone else who's going to entertain you for a bit. They're not some random comic being thrown on the show. They are with me. Be kind." I don't say it that literally, but that's the *subtext*. Since the backstage of this place was actually upstairs (and was also connected to someone's apartment), I had to introduce Ken from a microphone that they dragged into the parking lot. The show was great; it was quite full and the laughs bounced nicely from the low ceilings. Didn't stick around long after because I'd decided to catch a train back to New York. While we were about to pull away the promoter ran out. He needed to tell me something. "I calculated your pay wrong." It turned out I was getting half the amount I was originally quoted. I get it. You're deducting a little something for your janitorial services.

APRIL 30, 2015—BETHLEHEM, PENNSYLVANIA
STEELSTACKS

This was the makeup date for the snowed-out February show. I had Doogie Horner opening again, and things got off to an awkward start. He came to pick me up at the scheduled time. We were about to leave when he got a phone call. "It's my wife. She's locked out. I have to go back to help her."

"Where do you live again?"

"Queens," he said.

"She can't get a locksmith?" I asked, because I like asking obvious questions that should be asked.

After a few more awkward calls to his wife, he said, "I have to go back. It's my wife."

Yes, Doogie, I know it's your wife. Wives can call locksmiths, too.

I asked Doogie how long it would take for him to get home and come back to me. He gave me an estimate of about thirty or forty minutes, which I knew was a fantasy. It would be about an hour each way. But I agreed to let him go *save* her. I got out of the car and started walking, probably to a coffee shop. About forty steps into my stroll, I was overtaken with a specific type of anger, the kind I get when I feel like I caved when confronted with a dilemma because I feel guilty. Like when I'm leaving one of my shows with a group of friends, and some hanger-on/borderline stalker asks if they can join us and I say yes. I did a show in Chicago once. I had a few friends there; the hanger-on was there with his friends. We talked openly about where we were headed after the show. I ended up at a table with a group of friends on either side of me. I realized, *These people to my left all know each other; same with the people to my right. But this guy in the middle trying to interject? No one knows him.* He just followed us there. And I didn't stop it. It's always fascinating when someone like that, who is socially awkward, also manages to do something so presumptuous and ballsy. I wanted to move on to another bar; we did a quick "Good-bye, nice meeting you!" to this guy, to which he responded, "Are you guys going somewhere else? I was hoping to tag along." We moved on without him.

But back to Doogie. Before I even made it to a coffee shop, I called him and said, "I can't wait for you to go to Queens and come back." My plan was to get to Bethlehem a few hours early so I could check out the town. I hadn't been able to do this last time because of the snow. I didn't want to arrive right before the show. "Please see if your wife can just get a locksmith." He said he'd call me back. I hung up, feeling satisfied with my decision. I figured she wasn't in danger; she was just locked out. Getting a locksmith is just one of those things you need to experience once when you live in New York. I remember leaving my apartment years ago to get a coffee at the deli (before my *serious coffee awakening*). As the front door slammed, I knew I had locked myself out. I called a locksmith. He came over with a little square of Mylar-like material and wriggled it around for about two seconds. The door shot open like it had been kicked by a detective. We walked upstairs to my apartment door and repeated the process. The whole transaction took about three minutes, and I sat there enjoying my dollar deli coffee that cost me $120.

Doogie called me back and said he'd arranged for a locksmith. He drove back to my apartment entrance. This was good news, but I still felt nervous. Was I a jerk for not letting him go home? Or did I assert myself in a healthy way rather than making a guilt-based decision? Were we about to drive two hours in awkward silence? I approached the car and opened the door, and he was immediately apologetic. I knew the next couple of hours in the car wouldn't be tense, and more important, it made me feel comfortable enough to talk about this incident onstage a few hours later.

I chose the Hotel Bethlehem for this trip. It was downtown, so there were restaurants and shops within walking distance, including a cigar bar with outdoor seating. I'm surprised this is legal.

I stopped at a restaurant and had a salad with *cinnamon vinaigrette*. I love Atomic Fire Balls, but not sure why I thought that would work for a salad dressing.

SteelStacks is the old Bethlehem Steel factory. It's an event space that has a few different rooms. I was in a room usually used for movies (I guess that would be called a movie theater). Really fun crowd. Doogie did his set, then introduced me. I immediately launched into the story of how his wife locked herself out and how we almost left late because he didn't want to get a locksmith. "So Doogie actually expected me to wait for him while he helped his wife get in the house! Hilarious!"

Giving my opening act a public beating with his family in the audience was quite a treat.

I have a bit in my act about being a picky eater and I usually preface it by asking if anyone in the audience is a picky eater. A guy volunteered that he was a picky eater because he doesn't like the taste of cumin. "Oh, that's gotta be rough. It limits you to only ninety-nine point nine percent of all foods."

A nice couple approached me at the merch table, and they told me they were the parents of my friend Tim Heidecker. Tim and I met when I hosted and produced a comedy series, along with David Cross and Jon Benjamin, called Tinkle, which had a nice run at a rock venue called Pianos on the Lower East Side. We'd book a variety of acts—standup, character pieces. Tim and his partner Eric Wareheim would show short videos they made under the name Tim and Eric. They went on to create several shows for Adult Swim on the Cartoon Network. Over the years, Tim and I somehow developed one of those faux-contentious relationships where you spend a good percentage of the time insulting each other. I remember posting an insult directed at him on my Tumblr page (I just went through every post on my Tumblr page and couldn't find it, but I imagine it was something along the lines of "You're not funny"). He got me back big by writing a song called "Todd Barry Is an Idiot" and getting Aimee Mann to record it Have a listen: https://soundcloud .com/laughspin/aimee-mann-sings-todd-barry-is. Whenever someone introduces themselves after a show and explains we have a connection, I'm immediately relieved I didn't get into an onstage tussle with them. I imagine getting that call: *"Todd, it's Tim. Tim Heidecker. Did you have my mom thrown out of your show last night?"*

"She wouldn't stop texting during the show, Tim! She was in the fifth row! I warned her!"

After the show we met up with Doogie's little brother at the Bookstore Speakeasy, which we went to on the first trip. There was a twenties jazz band playing called the Red Hot Ramblers. They played a song called "My Girl's Pussy." I Googled this song and found out it's from 1931. I imagine that was a pretty saucy song back then, and I guess I was supposed to break out into an "Oh, that's naughty" smile every time they sang "pussy." But since I'm America's number one XXX-rated comic, you're gonna have to try just a *little* bit harder to shock me!

I stopped at a coffee shop called the Wise Bean the next morning and spoke to the proprietor, a sweet woman named Joan, who became even sweeter when I asked, "What is the Wi-Fi password?"

"Stormtrooper."

Thank you, Joan!

ARLINGTON CINEMA & DRAFTHOUSE

I sat on a train to DC, pretty excited that I was staying at the Westin hotel near the P. F. Chang's in Arlington. If you've never been to a P. F. Chang's, it's an Americanized Chinese restaurant chain. The restaurants are huge, like the size of a TGI Fridays, and the waitstaff also look like they work at TGI Fridays. The food isn't authentic, but neither was the food at the Chinese place in Florida where I worked as a dishwasher/delivery guy/busboy when I was seventeen. The highlight of this job was getting a call on a day off from my friend Steve, who also worked there, to tell me "Rip Taylor just walked into the restaurant" (Rip Taylor is a flamboyant comedian who was in town opening for Sammy Davis Jr. I was in my car headed to the restaurant within five minutes. Seeing Rip Taylor eating by himself in a strip-mall Chinese restaurant in suburban South Florida gave me an early glimpse of loneliness on the road). I love P. F. Chang's. I was about to check into a hotel that was within walking distance of their Arlington location. Well, get ready to cry, because, as it turns out—and I'm surprised no one warned me about this—there are *two* Westins in Arlington, and one of them is *not* near a P. F. Chang's. In fact it was not near anything. I eventually did find a place to eat, but I don't even remember where. If I'd eaten at P. F. Chang's, I would've remembered, and I would've *told all*: I would've shared great details about what I ordered, the spice level, the number of rice refills, etc. My loss is your loss.

I was able to sit in the "quiet car" on Amtrak, the car where people allegedly don't make loud calls or engage in loud conversation. I usually take Amtrak from Penn Station, where the boarding process is so tense, I'm often too panicked to figure out where the quiet car is, and I always regret it. But sometimes I *do* find it, and still regret it, because people don't seem to understand the "quiet" part. I think I summed up my feelings about this subject in my wonderful tweet from May 20, 2011:

> If you ride Amtrak, they have 1 "quiet" car, and 25 cars where you can have a conference call about your company's web site.

My shows were at the Arlington Cinema & Drafthouse, one of those movie theaters with a full bar and kitchen and table-side service. They generally show movies but also have a regular well-curated live comedy lineup. The people who run it treat comedians right. I remember the first time I played there, they handed me a check, with some cash they referred to as "a little walking-around money." This was a first.

The room isn't designed for standup comedy, but it usually works well. The only problem I had was with the section up front. It's like an orchestra pit sunk below the other seats, and people sitting there don't feel part of the show, so they talk. One night there was an awful man sitting up front who wouldn't shut up. I warned him repeatedly. At some point he stood up and pulled a $50 bill from his wallet and tried to hand it to me, which made me want to kick him in the face, like he's just going to wave me off with a fifty. I should have had him thrown out at that point. Instead I took his money, walked up to the mic, and said, "Does anyone want fifty dollars?" A young woman walked up and I handed her the bill. I hope she bought something nice for herself, because I felt dirty taking it.

But since that incident, they've stopped seating that front section unless there are no other seats available, and there's a big security guy planted near the stage.

I got to Arlington the day before the show. My friend Mac Mc-Caughan, the guy I ate pizza with in Durham (yes, the musician who was late), was doing a solo show in DC at a music venue called the Black Cat. I sent Mac a text that said, *VIP ALERT: Todd Barry + Brendan Canty tonight.* Brendan Canty is the drummer for seminal punk band Fugazi. I befriended him and Fugazi singer Ian MacKaye after doing a joke about them in my act and on *Letterman.* (Fugazi were famous for their integrity, which included charging only $6 for their shows. I respect integrity, too, but I will also make fun of it in exchange for money.)

So the three of us met up at the Black Cat and watched Mac's show. Ian said I should stop by the Dischord house the next day, a house in Arlington that was the former home to some of the band and Dischord, their record label. Now it serves as an archive for Fugazi memorabilia. I got to the house and made a weird social choice. He offered me some iced green tea, and I asked, "Is it good?" *Is it good? I'm asking if the iced tea he offered is good? Am I "vetting" this guy's iced tea? Who talks to people like that? That's not very PUNK!* I don't know what I meant to say, but it certainly wasn't "Is it good?" so I apologized like I just accused him of being a *corporate rocker*.

Ian showed me some cool stuff, including notebooks where he kept handwritten tour logs that included specific details like how much they got paid and even how much they spent on Cokes in a particular city. I asked him if Arlington qualified as a *secondary market*. He said it did.

I'm not sure why I questioned that. Maybe I was thrown off by the two Westins.

MAY 21, 2015—WINNIPEG, MANITOBA
THE PARK THEATRE

The plan was to take a super-early (7:00 a.m.!) flight to Winnipeg the day before my show. It was my first trip there, and I wanted to poke around the city, then go to my hotel to watch the final episode of *The Late Show with David Letterman*. I'd done standup on the show eight times, and when I was eighteen, I actually made an appearance by phone during the "viewer mail" segment of his NBC show. (It's true. Find the clip on youtube.com/toddbarryvideos.)

This plan changed when I got asked to film a scene for Aziz Ansari's Netflix show *Master of None*. I'd already filmed a few earlier episodes and given the producers the dates I wasn't available. I guess I left May 20 open in case they needed me. When I didn't hear back, I booked a flight for that day and didn't let them know. Well, they eventually asked me to work that day. They had a location already set and couldn't revolve around my schedule. This meant taking a later flight, so I could film my scene in the morning. I would miss the

Letterman finale, but I was DVR-ing it, so I just accepted the situation like a pro.

As with most of my acting roles, I was handed the role on *Master of None* because I knew someone involved in the project. I'm lucky that I have a few friends who are more ambitious than me and throw me little bones on their projects. These usually involve me playing a guy named Todd who works at a store and is kind of a wiseass. The exception to this is the movie *The Wrestler*, where I played a guy named Wayne who worked at a store and was kind of a wiseass. I have mixed feelings about acting. I like being *on set* (I used to say "on *the* set") and like that there are tables of free food. I like getting residual checks for work I did eight years ago. It's the demand on my time that sometimes frustrates me. Not that I work crazy-long hours, but things constantly change with movie and TV shoots, and you have to be ready to adjust your schedule to fit theirs. I don't always want to do that. But as I just said, you get free food and checks for work you did eight years ago. And in a lot of these projects, they give me the freedom to *run wild* with the script. I remember a chaotic scene in *The Wrestler* where Mickey Rourke's character Randy "the Ram" cuts himself on the meat grinder at the supermarket deli where I played his boss. There was lots of screaming and blood, and after one of the takes, I asked the director, Darren Aronofsky, if I could ad-lib. He said, "Don't censor yourself." I guess he gave the same direction to Mickey, because at some point he threw a big box of foil that hit my back. That wasn't in the script.

My flight was delayed and I had a horrific trip through customs in Toronto, including *slightly* losing my cool with an airport security officer when he wanted me to empty my pockets after I'd already walked through the scanner. It seemed unnecessary, so I kind of pulled my wallet out and slammed it on the belt. (If you witnessed this you'd probably say it was the gentlest *slamming* in history.) He gave me a look that made me realize he had the power to ruin my trip. That's about as violent as I get.

The Mere Hotel. Winnipeg, Manitoba.

I made it to Winnipeg and was greeted with a heavenly sight: the beautiful chill boutique hotel I'd selected. The promoter had originally booked me at an airport hotel. I was baffled. Why would I want to stay at the airport? He said because comics like the convenience. I guess it's convenient if you want to sightsee and eat all your meals at the airport. But I did see his point: there are comics who stay in their rooms all day, so they might as well be near the airport. I do not respect these comics. They lack my *Anthony Bourdain–like* sense of adventure.

The hotel was called the Mere. It was a beautiful two-story building completely covered in multicolored lights. If you drove past it you'd think it was a museum of contemporary art. And it was quiet.

The problem sometimes with staying in *cool* hotels is that some of them seem tranquil until I return after my show and find that they have a shitty nightclub attached, with a line of shitty people waiting to get in. Then you go up to your room and put in the earplugs that the hotel placed on your nightstand since they won't turn the music down. But none of that was an issue at the Mere. The only sound I could hear was the clacking of my laptop keys as I searched Yelp for coffee shops.

The next morning I went for a walk and discovered that Winnipeg was way more happening than I'd been told. My friend Courtney lives there and always said it was a dump, so that's what I was prepared for. But there were cool old buildings and a great coffee place called Parlour. I eventually met up with Courtney and we walked around to a place called the Forks, which is like a big food and shopping compound that's apparently the biggest tourist attraction in Winnipeg. We were hungry, and one of our dining options was a place called the Old Spaghetti Factory, the type of place you'd see on the road but never go into because "it's a chain." But you knew if you *did* eat there, you'd love every bite. I decided to embrace my desire to eat at the Old Spaghetti Factory and I wasn't disappointed. I ordered some pasta with pesto. (I don't recall ever hearing about pesto when I was a kid. I think it was invented in 1987.)

We walked around a bit more, then I took a city bus back to the Mere. I like taking public transportation when I'm in a new city. Feels gritty. Makes it seem like I'm super down-to-earth. Like the time I saw Henry Winkler on the subway. He wasn't even wearing a hat!

I was excited about my show that night. It was sold out in advance, probably because I'd never been to Winnipeg before, so they weren't tired of me.

Park Theatre. Winnipeg, Manitoba.

I did have one situation that I resolved before I got to town. I looked on the theater's website and noticed they were selling "VIP booths" to my show. This bummed me out, starting with the word "VIP." The deal was for one price you could get a table for six and twenty drink tickets, and you'd get to cut the line. If you asked me what two factors are bad for a comedy show I'd say drunkenness and big groups. Twenty drinks for six people might not sound like a lot, but you figure one person is not going to drink their allotment of 3.33 drinks, so that leaves the potential for someone having four or five drinks in two hours, which is enough to make a person turn ugly, and if you factor in these people cut the line and think of themselves as VIPs, well, that only makes things worse. (FULL DISCLOSURE: I'm a VIP.) I told my agent about this and they took the fancy booths off sale. I don't think the venue meant any ill will by offering them, and I'm sure I was the first and last person to complain.

The show was quite a *barnburner*. Super-lively crowd, including a guy who, during the "picky eater" segment, claimed he didn't "eat anything that grows in the ground." *We get it, you're a big meat guy. No vegetables for you! They grow in the ground!*

I performed for about an hour, said good night, then heard a special kind of applause. It was beyond polite-with-a-few-"woo-hoos" applause. This was "Oh shit, they want me to do an encore" applause. There are very few encores when you're doing comedy shows at my level. I don't even have an encore *locked and loaded*. The good news is that if you're getting an encore you've already won. It's not like people will be walking out going, "That was a great show, until he stunk up the place with that encore!" You just walk back out, scramble to remember a couple of jokes you didn't do during the set, insult a few people, then say good night again. And that's what I did.

SPACE

I wasn't sure if Evanston, Illinois, was truly a secondary market, but it sounded like one when I booked it. It turns out it's quite close to Chicago, but sometimes that doesn't mean anything. Years ago I did shows in Schaumburg, Illinois, also close to Chicago, and people there said playing Schaumburg instead of Chicago was like playing another planet. But most entertainers, including me, usually play Chicago.

But let's get to what made this gig great: the best greenroom ever. If I were nineteen (or one of those people who talk like they're nineteen) I would've written "The. Best. Green. Room. Ever." It was pretty amazing. Not like "This works fine as a greenroom," but more like "I could move in here and not change anything." Big, clean, and stylishly decorated. My usual definition of a good greenroom is: It has a bathroom that may or may not lock. And there's soap. I occasionally play places that don't even have a backstage bathroom, which sometimes means the only preshow pee option involves walking through the audience before the show starts. I'm a big *mystique* guy. I don't want to walk through the audience of people waiting to see me. So if it's by the stage, I will do whatever it takes to avoid it, even if that means just hanging out in the venue office or the back of the club until showtime and using the bathroom at a nearby restaurant.

The hand soap situation at SPACE was quite impressive. Not just that they had any, which is always a nice surprise, but it was that high-end Mrs. Meyer's stuff that comes in scents like basil and geranium. If that wasn't a warm enough welcome, there was also a cabinet attached to the wall where they had a big refill bottle. After the *traumatic* New England filthy-bathroom shows, this was a change I deserved.

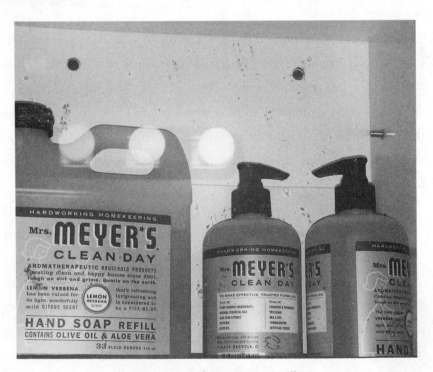

Backstage soap cabinet. Evanston, Illinois.

Within the sprawling, loftlike dressing room was another room with its own bathroom and a big TV, which I assumed was the headliner's dressing room. This was a nice bonus because I had four opening acts that night, so it would've been quite crowded. Usually I prefer just one, but these comics were from the Lincoln Lodge, a long-running Chicago comedy showcase, and they were presenting me in Evanston. They were a friendly bunch, and not annoying.

I did two shows that night at SPACE. I really don't like doing two shows in one night, because you decompress from the first show, then in like an hour you have to *reignite the passion* and start over again for the second show. I don't want to *reignite the passion*. I just want to go get something to eat. I realize many people work fifty hours a week, and don't get applause and free food and drink. I don't bring this up beacause I want you to to feel sorry for me, and really, if I play your town feel free to come to the second show. I'm a pro. You'll never know I'm not having a good time.

JUNE 3, 2015—TEL AVIV, ISRAEL

ZAPPA

The day I left for Tel Aviv I posted this on Twitter and Facebook:

RESEARCH I DID FOR TODAY'S TRIP TO ISRAEL:

1. *Looked at Jerusalem Wikipedia entry*
2. *Googled "best Thai food in Tel Aviv"*

A stranger responded:

Remember Apartheid? That still exists in Israel.

Oh shit, you didn't like my Thai food joke? I got this uneasy feeling that it was morally wrong for me to go to Israel. Even though I'm perceived as being insanely intelligent, I'm pretty weak on the subject of foreign affairs. But I have made plenty of business decisions based on ethics. I was once offered an extra $500 if a cigarette company could pass out samples at my show. That was an easy no. The Israel gig was more confusing to me. I asked some of my smart friends and nobody really said, "You shouldn't go there, Todd." And I know plenty of kind, liberal, and even activist comics who have performed in Israel, so I figured it was okay.

I was hoping my experience in Israel would be similar to the one I had with Australia. I remember getting booked in Melbourne in 2004. Until that point I'd never thought much about Australia or had much curiosity about visiting. Then I got there and I loved it. I had the same feeling about visiting Israel. I'm Jewish, but it wasn't on my list of must-visit countries.

I arrived a few days before my two scheduled shows—one in Tel Aviv, another the next day in Herzliya. The promoter, a super-nice and accommodating guy named Avisar, greeted me at the airport. I was pretty tired, especially since I flew coach on the eleven-hour flight. I'd been waitlisted for an upgrade to business class, and when I asked about it at the airport the gate agent said, "Anything could happen . . ." The unspoken second part of that was "as long as it involves you flying coach."

I checked into my hotel and saw that my name was misspelled in the reservation. I was more visibly upset about this than I needed to be, and the woman at the front desk, who had that intimidating vibe I feel from some Israeli people, looked at me like I'd scolded her. She got her revenge later on when I locked myself out of my room. She gave me my new key and said, "I guess you make mistakes, too." This got a huge smile from me. I've never done such a severe 180 on how I felt about someone. I was in love.

I'm glad she and I worked out our differences, because I ended up switching rooms three times over the next few days—a new record for me. One of the rooms had a bad bed; another had a bathroom so small, if you were sitting on the toilet and moved forward an inch, your chest would touch the sink; and the third room had a broken air conditioner.

There was a welcome dinner with the promoters and publicists my first night in Tel Aviv at a place called Herbert Samuel, which I was told was a "chef's restaurant." Most people would react with "Ooh, a chef's restaurant—chefs go there—that must be great!" I reacted with "Ooh, a chef's restaurant—chefs go there—get ready for a bunch of shit I won't eat." It turns out there was stuff I could eat, including . . . barbecued ribs! As in barbecued *pork* ribs. I knew there were a lot of secular people in Israel, but I didn't expect my first meal to involve pork.

At some point, I found out my show in Herzliya was canceled. The owner of the clubs had a minimum sales target of 250. Ticket sales there were slower than Tel Aviv, but it was still on its way to being a crowd of 150 people in a 350-seat venue, which is not full, but more than enough to do a proper show where everyone had fun and makes money. They'd paid me for both shows in advance, so I didn't really argue, but it was weird to cancel a show because it's not absolutely full. It's not like they only sold six tickets.

The Tel Aviv show was emceed by Iris Bahr, an actor and performer who I'd met in New York years ago, and the opening act was Kobi Maimon, a popular Israeli comic who was doing his first-ever set in English.

The show was sold out, and I was a bit nervous. When you do a show overseas, there's *always* something that won't translate. You can go over your act in your head and anticipate a few of these things, but there are words and phrases they don't use, and you might not realize this until you're about to say one of them. I did a show in England once and was about to use the word "Dumpster." In a split second I had the worry *What if they don't use "Dumpster" here?* So I changed it to "bin" and the joke worked, and now I'm the biggest American comic in the UK. This is the type of thing to consider when you're doing a show in English-speaking countries but even more of an issue when performing in a place where English is their second language. I did a European tour in 2014 that included stops in Helsinki, Stockholm, Oslo, and Amsterdam. The crowds that showed up were so polite and appreciative, there was no problem with references they didn't get. I just had to *set the table* a bit. If I was about to touch on one of these subjects—like this amazing joke I do about Walgreens—I'd say, "I'm about to do a joke about Walgreens. Do you guys know what Walgreens is?" They would shake their heads. "Well, it's like a big drugstore. What's the name of the big drugstore here?" They would answer. Then I'd say, "Well, Walgreens is like that." And then I'd do the joke and they would laugh.

My favorite moment of the show was when I did some audience banter to set up a terrible joke I used to do about never seeing someone take a shit in the street in NYC, but seeing something worse (a couple having sex on the staircase). It usually gets a laugh, and maybe it's not a terrible joke, but there's always something in my act that I don't like, and it doesn't help that the joke is about a guy taking a shit. Anyway, I sometimes set it up (i.e., stall for time) by asking someone the worst thing they've ever witnessed in their city. I asked a guy up front, "What's the worst thing you've ever seen in Tel Aviv?" He fired back with "A cat raping a rat." Okay, well, at least you understood the question.

I'd planned to have one day off after my shows, but that turned into two because of the Herzliya cancellation. When I arrived in Tel Aviv, I thought, *This is really beautiful,* but I didn't feel uneasy; it wasn't *much* different from being in Miami or someplace like that. But then Avisar, Iris, and I drove to Jerusalem and I thought, *Well, I'm definitely in Israel.* I wasn't terrified, but there was an energy I wasn't completely comfortable with. I've never shot a gun in my life, so seeing all these men walking around with their fingers tapping triggers didn't help.

Wailing Wall. Jerusalem.

We walked through the endless Arab markets and went to the Wailing Wall, where I respected their "no pictures" policy. My yarmulke flew off my head at one point, which has happened all five times in my life I've worn one, including every indoor Bar Mitzvah I've been to. We were walking through a beautiful church when a long-haired hippie guy who I would describe as *Mr. Jerusalem* approached me. "Todd Barry! Can I get a picture?" I was surprised to get recognized at a church in Jerusalem. Even if I had a "no pictures" policy I'd say yes to this.

CROSSROADS
AT HAWAIIAN BRIAN'S

I've traveled for many years, yet Hawaii was on a long list of places I'd never visited, including:

Mexico
South America
China
Thailand
Africa
Germany
Portugal

I've heard exactly two negative things about Hawaii in my entire life. I don't remember who said the first one, or what they didn't like about it, I just remember them saying "I don't like Hawaii" and being shocked at hearing my first criticism of the most-loved place on earth. It was like when you meet one of those weirdos who claim they don't like cake. *Oh yeah, you don't like cake. Of course. What's to like about delicious, sweet cake? I get it!* The second negative comment came from a comic friend of mine who, after I told him I got booked there, just shrugged and said, "I don't really want to go to Hawaii." I won't mention the comic's name because there may be a comedy promoter reading this who will go, "I was about to book this guy in Hawaii, but if he won't appreciate it, then fuck him!" I'm not interested in taking work away from my friends (there was a time I was *very* into this, but not anymore).

I was excited to get booked in Hawaii to do just two shows over five days. My girlfriend of two and a half years had just broken up with me—I guess she got out before she *had to go to Hawaii*—so I thought this would be a good decompressing vacation.

I cashed in some frequent-flier miles to get a first-class upgrade, which I assumed meant I could go to the first-class lounge. If you've never been in a first-class lounge, it's like a breakfast buffet at a Hampton Inn, only in an airport. There's free food and drink, and unlike at the hotel breakfast buffet, you might see celebrities. (My two biggest sightings: Matthew McConaughey slumped in a chair wearing sunglasses in the British Airways lounge at Heathrow, and Jane Fonda, a few feet from me at the cookie table in the Air Canada lounge at the Vancouver airport. I left them both alone, because I *get it*.) It's also a place where you can see some of those *frequent-flier assholes* I mentioned in an earlier chapter. I was once at an airport where my flight was delayed many hours. I didn't have a first-class ticket, so I wasn't allowed in the lounge unless I bought a day pass for $50. I figured it was worth it since the delay was so long. I was in line at the check-in desk at the lounge inquiring about the pass, and I guess it was taking a while. The guy behind me in line yelled, "Is *he* a member?" The guy behind the desk asked, "Who?" The shithead in line pointed to me. I turned to him and said, "I'm buying a pass. Is that okay?" The miserable, unimportant *gentleman* didn't react. I guess he saw me in my T-shirt and thought I didn't "have what it takes" to enjoy unlimited coffee, free Wi-Fi, and snack mix. I'm not a big revenge guy, but I wanted to really lay into him. "What was it about the way I was standing in line that made you think it was okay to talk to me that way, while *pointing* at me?" But I didn't. Instead I waited for him to enter the lounge, then sat directly across from him shaking my head while making intense eye contact. He eventually got up and left.

I confidently walked through the United Club's glass doors at Newark airport and flashed my first-class ticket. The woman at the desk looked at it and said, "This lounge is only for international flights." *Huh? I'm flying to Hawaii. Yes, I know it's a state—but the flight is like four hours longer than a flight to Europe.* I still think the woman may have made a mistake by not admitting me, but I didn't argue much. I just turned around and headed for the exit—probably too angry for a guy who was being paid to tell jokes in Hawaii.

I used to do a bit in my act about someone who described Disney World to me as *too touristy*. That was my first impression of Honolulu. I saw a strip with lots of chain stores and was a little disappointed, but then, unlike at Disney World, I'd turn my head and see the most beautiful sky and water I'd ever seen in my life.

I walked around on the strip a bit, found a coffee shop. I asked the barista for food recommendations, and he responded, "I always like California Pizza Kitchen and Cheesecake Factory." I don't remember where I ended up eating, but it was something more *local*.

I roamed for a bit, then I was hit with that wonderful feeling: "Ooh, this is a pedicure town," a term I made up thirty seconds ago. Basically Hawaii seemed like a place for *leisure*, and I wanted it to feel like a vacation, so I went online and found a highly reviewed spa at the Westin hotel. They put me in a waiting room, which they called the Relaxation Room. It had a huge window and was directly on the beach; people were sunbathing five feet from me. I sat there eating trail mix and drinking iced tea, waiting to get my little toes pampered.

I'd heard there was a zoo directly behind my hotel. I wasn't sure if I should go to the zoo alone. I did that in Melbourne and felt like a weirdo. But Shane Price—the genial comic who'd booked me in Honolulu—told me my comedian friend Ian Edwards went to the zoo alone when he was in town, so I pictured my friend Ian walking around the zoo alone and thought, *Why not? How often is your hotel near a zoo?* So I went to the zoo alone, and felt even more alone when I realized there were no animals to keep me company. I don't know what was going on that day, but animal-wise, it was slim pickings. I eventually saw a lone giraffe, but I don't know where everyone else was hiding. A zoo without animals is like a Todd Barry show without a standing ovation.

That night Shane, a few other comics, and I ate dinner at a Honolulu institution called the Side Street Inn. After overordering plates of Hawaiian fried pork chop, chicken misoyaki, calamari, and local char siu fried rice, the waitress made the curious suggestion that we get "one more protein," so I think we got another chicken dish. After that Shane took me to an open mic night at a smaller bar within the same complex I was going to perform in. I thought it would be fun to check out the Hawaiian comedy scene, but it was a bit sad. It was a tiny audience, which is fine, but they were chatty, like there wasn't a show going on. I was angry and frustrated for the comics, so I left early. Shane drove me to Chinatown and showed me a statue of King Kamehameha (who apparently was a big Todd Barry fan!).

The day of the show a local comic named Jose volunteered to show me around the island. We drove to this luxurious hotel that had a pool filled with real live dolphins, better animal options than mine, and I was staying fifty feet from a zoo. Jose told me this hotel was where visiting celebrities stayed. *Um, hell-OH. Not all of them!*

My show was at venue called Crossroads at Hawaiian Brian's—essentially a pool hall with a separate concert space inside. We had to walk through the gym next door to enter. I doubt the audience used that route, so I'm guessing this was the *VIP* entrance.

Crossroads is mainly a rock club, so the stage was quite high and had a mosh pit/metal barricade in front of it. I prefer to have the audience seated right up to the edge of the stage, but I occasionally get this setup, which allows me to joke about the club having a "safety moat" that deters people from rushing the stage.

The audience felt like a mix of actual comedy fans and local curiosity seekers. But they were quite responsive, especially Shane, who had a big goofy laugh that threw off my timing so much, I had to stop and make fun of him a bit, which is understandable. Since I'm a comedian, you'd expect me to be distracted by laughs.

CHARLEY'S RESTAURANT AND SALOON

I arrived in the town of Paia, Maui, and faced a crisis: I couldn't start my laptop. It's an awful, frustrating feeling when I can't start my computer. I mean it's an awful feeling for me. I start thinking about the hassle of making a Genius Bar appointment, then going to the Apple Store, or using my phone to look up tech-support solutions. But after a few minutes of enraged fiddling, I can usually get it started. I think my fiddling was extra enraged this time because I had just checked into a two-bedroom suite in a beautiful beachfront inn in Maui, and now I was angry about a broken laptop. So I was mad about the computer and also mad about being mad. But it proved a point I always bring up when I get in a discussion about happiness. Let's say I'm talking to an actor. I say, "You could get cast in the role of a lifetime on Wednesday, but if you can't find your wallet on Thursday, that's all you'll be thinking about." They are usually floored with this amazing, sharp insight.

After failing to get my laptop started, I called Paul Chamberlain, who produces the Maui Comedy Festival and had brought me in as the first act in a new summer series. He picked me up at the airport and then bought me some nice fried shrimp at a lunch with his wife and two kids. I said, "Is there a Mac repair store we could go to? I can't get my laptop started." He said he knew of a place and drove me there. I sat in the passenger seat, beaming like I was in Hawaii.

Before we entered the Mac repair store, I had this feeling, *This guy is going to push two buttons and get this thing started. And if he does, how much is he going to charge for that?* I put the MacBook Air on the counter, and within five seconds I heard that little chime. "What do I owe you?" I asked with very little expectation of hearing a price. "There's no charge, I really didn't do anything." That was the right answer (and also what I should say after I have a bad show). And for you tech geeks who were guessing all along: yes, the PRAM needed to be reset.

That night I went out to Ho'okipa Beach with Paul; his wife, Kacky; and their kids. It was a little odd watching the sunset in Hawaii with a family you just met, but everyone was friendly, it was an amazing sunset, and there were turtles. A huge one had made it to shore, and it was actually taped off like a crime scene by the Hawaii Wildlife Fund. Later we found a monk seal that also made it to shore, also taped off, with a woman sitting there to guard it. I wanted to tell them the good news about my laptop, but I left them alone. They seemed very peaceful and I didn't want to get them all *stirred up.*

The next day we drove up to the summit of Haleakala National Park. It took over an hour to get up there, but it was worth it. Breathtaking views. It's weird to look at something that beautiful, then look at your watch and go, "I think I get it!"

There was a shaved-ice place I wanted to try, so we went over and got a little rainbow-colored treat that some people might call a sno-cone, although to be fair, it was in a bowl. I posted a picture of me eating it on Facebook, and some dude wrote, *The locals must have hated you.* I didn't respond, but I couldn't imagine what he was talking about. Did he think the locals would take a break from looking at the beautiful sky to *taunt* people over their frozen dessert choice?

Hawaiian drink options.

The show that night was at a place called Charley's Restaurant and Saloon, which looked like a place Jimmy Buffett would have played when he was starting out. They didn't really have a greenroom, so they said I could hang out in the back office. I had no problem with that, but they waited too long to run the air-conditioning, so it was boiling hot, which put me in a shit mood. Comedy and heat are not a good combination. There's a reason David Letterman had his studio so cold you could see your breath. I was told I could hang out on the patio of the adjacent restaurant but felt weird about sitting there when I wasn't a customer. I ended up lingering outside the side entrance to the club.

I'm not sure how most of the audience ended up at my show. There were only a handful of people I sized up as comedy nerds (a.k.a. my *meal tickets*), so I think it was mainly local curiosity seekers. The show was okay; I wasn't really *killing*, and I was dripping with sweat. It really tested my professionalism. There was a rather rambunctious older lady up front, who I'm going to call Dolores, because that's *very* close to her actual name. I think she had a few too many sauvignon blancs; she interrupted a few times like we were having a conversation. This happens from time to time. People forget you're on a stage and react like you're sitting across from them at dinner. Let's say you have a joke that begins with "So ice cream is delicious." They'll respond aloud, "Oh yes, it is!" Then you'll think or say, "Hey, I'm just trying to do my famous 'ice cream is delicious' bit, and I don't need your input." It was a rough thing to deal with because she wasn't mean, she just didn't know better. That's better than mean, but you feel more justified shutting down someone who's mean.

Before I left New York I'd gotten an e-mail from my comedian friend Kyle Kinane:

You're going to Maui. I never wanted to retire until I went there.

I don't think a lot about retirement (calm down, I have an IRA set up), but I'm not sure I agree with him. I'd worry that I'd get used to how beautiful it was, and then I'd be bored. I live in New York City and I get bored, and we have sno-cones here, too. I mean, I think we do. Shit, maybe we don't!

THE SAINT

In New York City, most of the clubs are showcase clubs, and you basically get paid pocket money (Twenty-five to thirty dollars for a fifteen-minute set during the week). New Jersey has a lot of comedy clubs and one-night bar shows you can headline and make actual money without traveling too far.

In all my New Jersey trips I'd never been to Asbury Park. I'd heard about a club called the Saint, which mainly booked bands, but also the occasional comedian. At first it was a club I associated with Bruce Springsteen, but then realized I was confusing it with the Stone Pony.

I arrived with my opening act, Joe Zimmerman, a comic I'd met in 2007 when he lived in North Carolina. He'd booked me years ago to do a comedy night at a wine bar in Charlotte. For some reason he asked me to do two shows on a Wednesday night. I've already mentioned I don't like doing two shows in one night, but I really don't like it when the audiences for both shows aren't even enough to fill one show, and it's extra weird on a Wednesday. There are still a few comedy clubs out there that have three-show Saturday nights. I've done a few of those, and often the third show has thirty people at it. I guess Joe's thinking for the Charlotte gig was *It's just a wine bar in Charlotte, we could* easily *fill two shows.* Well, they didn't. Or to be fair, I didn't. But it was worth it because now I can say I performed at a wine bar that also sold Jell-O shots.

We drove to New Jersey in Joe's 2003 Ford Focus that had 360,000 miles on it. We had both recently gone through breakups, so there was a lot of super-sensitive guy talk in the car. We pulled over at least six times to cry. That's not true, but it was good to bond over this topic. Joe told me about a dating app he was using called Bumble, where the woman has to initiate contact with the man. I explained to him that I was *way* too famous to be on a dating app and would be a victim of some bait-and-switch prank. But I love hearing dating stories. I advised him on one woman in particular who had insulted him during their chats. He seemed to be reluctant to continue contacting her, but I thought he should at least meet her. Maybe her insults were like the ones I hurl from the stage, flirtatious and harmless, and maybe if he met her, they'd hit it off. I e-mailed him when I was writing this and he sent me screenshots of the actual texts. This was one exchange:

BUMBLE WOMAN: I bet you perform with napkins in your armpits.

JOE: I've never broken a sweat in my life.

BUMBLE WOMAN: You're a comedian. Your sweats, like your ego, come already broken.

Sort of funny, but not if that's the dynamic they got locked into. Joe never went out with her.

We stopped at a rest stop for some food and I nearly got run over by a dude backing out of a parking space. It was one of those incidents that I would describe as a close call, but if you witnessed it, you would describe it as "The guy started backing out but then realized his mistake, and it was no big deal." But it triggered a recurring fantasy where I imagine people reacting to my death. I try to guess which celebrities would tweet things like *Todd Barry was a great comic and REALLY great guy!* and picture the non-celebs posting long paragraphs on Facebook. I think about them being sad, then I get sad. But truthfully, this really was a close call.

We made it to the club and were greeted by their effervescent staff, who were very friendly in a "We've had too much coffee" way. They shared a certain specific buzzy energy that I couldn't figure out.

I told them I didn't want anyone texting or filming me. They printed up some signs telling people not to use their phones.

A crowd of sixty-eight people showed up that night. It wasn't a huge venue, so it didn't look as dismal as that might sound. But when it's under a hundred I get a little bummed. Seriously, only sixty-eight people show up for a guy who is too famous to be on a dating app?

I do a joke about the time I spent $14 on one bar of soap. I did the opening line, "You have to splurge in life," then asked a guy up front what his last *splurge* was. There was a pause, and I knew what was coming: "I don't know what that word means." I felt bad, but also thought, *How do you not know what the word "splurge" means? Is my act that brainy? I can't use "splurge" onstage?* But I didn't want to make the guy feel bad, so I just said, "Oh, you don't know what it means? It's like when you spend a lot of money on something," then I finished the joke. I didn't *have* to take the super-sweet and compassionate route, but I did. And I taught him a new word. Maybe he was talking to someone the next day and said, "I'm glad I *splurged* on Todd Barry tickets last night!"

Toward the end of the show I noticed a woman sleeping in the crowd. I shouldn't admit this, but as far as people falling asleep at my shows, *this wasn't my first rodeo*. People fall asleep at my shows. People fall asleep at a lot of shows. I fell asleep at a strip club in West Palm Beach. I'm never really bothered by people falling asleep during my show. It doesn't necessarily mean they're bored with me. I've been told I have a "soothing" voice, so that might be it. Or maybe they had a rough day at work and shouldn't have gone out to begin with. There's also the possibility that they might find my act to be boring, so they fall asleep. It never bothers me. I'd rather have someone sleeping than talking. And part of the reason it doesn't bother me is, I always wake them up.

Because seriously, what the fuck are you doing sleeping at my show? So I woke this woman up and found that her little nap had refreshed her. She was suddenly quite chatty. We exchanged some mutually feisty banter that probably went something like this:

"Hey, sleepyhead. What's your name?"

"Lisa."

"Rough day at work, Lisa? What do you do?"

"I'm in public relations."

"Oooh. Sounds grueling!"

As I was getting ready to leave the club, I noticed a camera mounted near the sound board. "Did you guys film my show?" I asked one of the people who put up signs saying not to film the show. "Yeah, we film all the shows for security reasons." I was a bit incredulous that they would do that themselves, but they handed me the DVDs and said there wasn't a copy stored anywhere else. I have no idea where I put those DVDs and I probably never will.

Joe and I found a brightly lit Korean taco place, then headed back to the Holiday Inn Express in nearby Neptune, New Jersey.

The next morning I met my musician friend Nicole Atkins for coffee. She lives in Asbury Park but couldn't come to the show because she was stuck in the studio. If I were a musician, I'd use that excuse all the time. "Sorry I couldn't come to your wedding, man. Stuck in the studio!" But I really think she was stuck in the studio. We went to her regular coffee shop. I pointed out that a lot of the clientele seemed like aging punks. She laughed and said, "All the old punks moved in and started soap stores."

THE STRESS FACTORY

I returned to the Stress Factory for an unprecedented second show in the same year, or as some people might say: *by popular demand.*

The most memorable thing about this night was throwing Joe Zimmerman out of the dressing room. I know, it sounds dramatic, but it wasn't. There was no brawl. No argument. He didn't do anything wrong. It's just that he was hungry and I have a disorder called *misophonia.*

From WebMD: *Misophonia, also known as selective sound sensitivity syndrome, starts with a trigger. It's often an oral sound—the noise someone makes when they eat, breathe, chew, yawn, or whistle.*

I diagnosed myself with this disorder (I can't imagine a doctor testing for it by eating Pringles in front of you), and I don't have a big problem with breathing or yawning sounds, so please, breathe and yawn away. But eating and chewing sounds, oh man, that's what gets me. And whistling? Also awful. (I've been in coffee shops where the barista starts whistling, which, *in concert* with my raw coffee nerves, makes it difficult to get any of my wonderful writing done.)

I share this syndrome with my friend Sarah Silverman. (Not name-dropping; I've know her since she was nineteen, we used to live in the same building, and yes, I'm also name-dropping.) I remember doing a set at a small room in the East Village. She was standing in the back while I was onstage, but then I noticed she was gone. Later she mentioned she walked out because she was standing next to a woman whose gum chewing was unbearable. Luckily for Sarah, at some point in the show, I'd stood next to that same woman and experienced it myself, so all was forgiven. Another time, we were eating in a mostly empty restaurant near our apartment. They sat us next to a group of people who, in retrospect, were only guilty of the crime of *eating in a restaurant*, but everything they did, every little clink of their forks, reverberated through the restaurant. We stared at each other, then moved to a different table.

The acoustics of a dressing room are not ideal for eating and are a constant source of anxiety for me, and backstage food is the noisiest. Vegetable trays, chips, nuts. So there's always a chance the opening act will walk in and bite into a baby carrot, and the crunch will shoot through me like a gunshot (although a gunshot would at least be interesting to experience). I don't usually say anything. Sometimes I'll leave my own dressing room so some guy can smack his dumb lips while eating Doritos.

I decided to go for the classic "no more Mr. Nice Guy" approach in New Brunswick. We sat in the tiny dressing room. The menus were down. The chicken fingers were sizzling in the fryer. I took a deep breath. "Hey, Joe, I'm kind of weird about hearing people eat. Do you think you can eat out in the showroom?" His reaction was not quite hurt, but also not "Of course, I understand." I felt a little bad as he walked out and sat in the back of the club. But later he told me he preferred eating there. More room to spread out. What I'm saying is, I did him a favor.

During the show a guy stomped his foot. This didn't trigger my misophonia, just my curiosity.

"What are you doing?"

"I killed a spider," he said.

You killed a spider? During my show? I'm not sure what would compel someone to do that. Was the spider talking? What an interesting impulse to follow through on. I once did a weird show in an alley in Melbourne, Australia. A rat walked by while I was performing and I didn't try to kill it.

After the show, I went to get paid and found out there were sixty-eight people in the audience. Same number as in Asbury Park. Oh, New Jersey!

THE MILL

In 2012 I did a show in Iowa City that was so good I often use it as an example of how you can have a great show outside of a major city. It was at a place called the Mill, a barebones seated music venue with a restaurant attached. I walked onstage, said a few words, and got this "*Ooh!* This is going to be good" feeling. There were no pockets of resistance. I don't mean they were an *easy* crowd that would laugh at anything (that would be *terrible*). It was this feeling of "Oh, they're here to enjoy my show." What I'm saying is there were no assholes.

The 2015 show was also at the Mill. It's set up pretty nice for comedy: low ceiling, seats packed up front, and another bonus: a Sheraton hotel right next door. Just head out of the kitchen exit, walk through an alley, and you're *home*. I love staying within walking distance of the venue. It's not like I say, "Thank you, good night," then run out of the venue, but I love having that option. I think Dead Kennedys summed up my feelings best with the title of their 1987 album, *Give Me Convenience or Give Me Death*.

I was all ready to stay at the Sheraton again, but I was burned by the "There's something going on that week" phenomenon, which occurs when you are all prepared to book a hotel room, or play a show with a big crowd, but you find out there's an event in town that stands in your way. There could be a big football game that night, which turns an $80-a-night Holiday Inn into a $350-a-night Holiday Inn. Or there was that time I did a show somewhere, and they mentioned that attendance might be affected because the Spin Doctors were doing a free show in a nearby parking lot.

This time I had something called RAGBRAI to deal with. "RAGBRAI" stands for "the Register's Annual Great Bicycle Ride Across Iowa." It's a one-week noncompetitive ride across Iowa that somehow also includes a Cheap Trick concert. I don't think it always includes Cheap Trick, but it would be funny if it did (like they canceled the whole ride if Cheap Trick wasn't available). So this was all going on in town while I was there, which meant my favorite Sheraton was booked up. I ended up staying at a Marriott in nearby Coralville. I arrived there and found they were hosting a group more intriguing than the cyclists: the annual AnimeIowa convention. Yep, Iowans interested in Japanese animation roamed around my hotel, dressed up as their favorite characters. There was even a table of makeup-removal bags and washcloths set up near the elevator. You will not find that perk at the Sheraton.

For Your Convenience

Makeup removal wash cloths and extra garbage bags have been placed on the elevator landing of each floor.

I got to town the day before the show and walked to a place called Waterstreet Coffee, where a pour-over coffee is only $2.20. If you've never had a pour-over coffee, you should try it. They put the freshly ground coffee in this cone contraption and slowly pour water over it. It takes a long time, but there's something romantic about the craftsmanship. And the pour-over there was cheaper than a drip coffee in New York.

That night I went to a pub and restaurant called Sanctuary. I'm sure somewhere in the world there's a loud dance club with that name, but this place was quiet. I ordered a pizza with sausage and jalapeños. If you like those two ingredients (and also pizza), I highly recommend the combination.

I went back to the coffee place the next the day, for what turned out to be the second of three trips there. Yes, that's just seven trips away from a free coffee, if they follow the typical conventions of coffee shop punch cards.

The Johnson County Historical Society Museum was right next to the Marriott, so I decided to give it a look. The $5 admission also got you into the Antique Car Museum of Iowa in the same building. I went in; got my usual panicky, overwhelmed museum feeling; and checked out dioramas of Iowa history, some maps, and a cool old Coke machine from 1960. I'm not a big *car guy* at all, but I am a big "Once I start taking pictures, I don't stop" guy, so I grabbed about fifty shots of old automobiles from the early 1900s and a display titled "Hubcaps from 1909 through 1930."

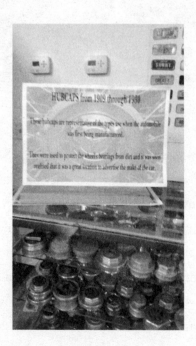

The show that night was fine, but not as good as my first trip to Iowa City. Or maybe it *was* just as good, but I had high expectations from that first trip. I should've asked Cheap Trick to open for me.

COMEDY CLUB ON STATE

When I first played Madison in 2010, the show almost didn't happen. I had received an e-mail from the booker days before the date, expressing concern with ticket sales. He said the club owner was worried that only thirty people would show up (it was the Tuesday after Labor Day) and it wouldn't be worth it for me. I wrote back:

> I'd much rather do a good show for 30 people than have to announce that it's canceled. That way people will leave feeling good about me and the club.
>
> And I also think people tend to buy tickets for comedy shows at the last minute, especially on a holiday weekend, so there's a good chance that more than 30 people will show up.
>
> So don't worry about me. I want to do the show.

After all that he responded, *Okay*, and I thought the matter was settled. The day before the show I was in a car somewhere in Illinois, and I got an e-mail from the booker on my BlackBerry:

they want to cancel..only 5 tickets sold!!!!

The above was cut and pasted from the actual e-mail. There really were four exclamation points after that little statement. Nearly one for each ticket sold!!!!

The booker's message made me angry. If I was headlining a five-thousand-seat opera house, and there were only a hundred tickets sold two weeks before the show, it would be reasonable to cancel because the promoter would lose a ton of money. But this was a two-hundred-fifty-seat comedy club and it was the day before the show. I'd already taken a plane to be in the area. I'd received e-mails from people who were driving a long way to get there. I just loved my fans too much to cancel!

So I got in touch with my manager, and the show went on for maybe seventy or so people. I know the club gave away some free tickets, but the people who showed up were great, and the people who worked at the club seemed happy.

I returned to the Comedy Club on State in 2015. By now it was enjoying a reputation as one of the best clubs in the country. It was packed, and when the emcee announced me, the applause was real "Springsteen in Newark" kind of shit. I had declined the club's offer to record my show, but I wish I hadn't. It would be worth a listen just to hear a person in the audience whose two-item list of foods they didn't like was "liver and coconut."

After the show my opening act Tyler Menz took me to an open mic night going on at a place called Great Dane. We walked over there and it seemed like a good time. I was tempted to do a set, but then I became fixated on a dude in the crowd who was eating wings. (You might know where this is headed.) He slurped each finger after *every bite* like he was sucking out viper venom. I looked at the woman he was with. She seemed unfazed even though this was going on inches from her face. *How is she not bothered by this?* It made me hate her, too. I mean, does she deal with this every time they go eat? If I owned a wing restaurant and this guy came in and ate like that, I'd hand him a stack of napkins and say, "Use these, or leave." And this was going on during a *show*. How can you be so oblivious? Some people have misophonia, you know!

NIKON AT
JONES BEACH THEATER

I got booked on a couple of stops on the Oddball Comedy and Curiosity Festival, a summer comedy tour of amphitheaters in its third year that featured a huge, rotating lineup of top comedians, such as Amy Schumer, Aziz Ansari, Nick Kroll, Michael Che, and Anthony Jeselnik. I never got asked to do the first two years, so I got a little more *proactive* (hate that word, possibly the first time I've used it) and sent a Facebook message to the promoter, whom I knew well and who had booked me many times at the Punch Line in San Francisco. I didn't feel *entitled* to be on the tour, but I had this sick feeling that I hadn't been asked because they thought I couldn't *handle* it, because I'm *low energy*—the type of nonissue that's burdened me in the past, even playing smaller places. But I had just done Madison Square Garden with Louis (I think I told you this already), so I mentioned that in my Facebook message and told him the show went well and that I was *arena-ready*.

They gave me two dates on the tour, Jones Beach on Long Island and Holmdel, New Jersey.

I remember seeing the singer Joe Jackson perform at Jones Beach many years ago. The winds were strong and the stage lights were swinging precariously above the band. I remember seeing the drummer look up at them, making a face like he knew this could be his last show.

I expected to go on first in the Oddball lineup (because I'm *low energy*, or maybe not as famous as the other acts) and that is the slot they gave me. It's not ideal, but it's a big nerve-racking gig, so part of me wanted to get it over with. Also, I liked going on before the sun went down so I could see the crowd. Some comics like it pitch-black when they go on. I prefer to *face the enemy*.

The show was hosted by Jeff Ross, who I've known since he went by his real name, Jeff Lifschultz. Jeff kind of blew up from doing Comedy Central roasts, and that soon became his *thing*. He went onstage at Jones Beach armed with something called a *roast cam* hooked up to his phone. He would find someone in the crowd and aim his phone at them. They would be projected on a giant screen, and then he would proceed to insult them. It was definitely funny, but not necessarily something I wanted to follow.

But as you gain experience as a comic and do a wide variety of shows, you learn there are different sets of rules for different situations. For these two Oddball shows, I knew I was going to walk out onstage and there would be a bit of chaos. I don't mean people losing their minds at the sight of me. I mean it was still early in the night, so people would be finding their seats, getting up to go buy a beer, maybe throwing around a beach ball, etc. In these situations I just try to think of the numbers. A few years prior, I opened for Ricky Gervais at a five-thousand-seat theater in New York. Ricky insisted on starting the show on time (actually three minutes late, which is the same as on time). This meant half the audience wouldn't be there when I was onstage. But I just thought, *Well, there are only two thousand people here now, but how often do I play for two thousand people?* It was the same at Jones Beach. I just looked out, found pockets of people who were focused, and performed for them. I ignored the people playing Frisbee.

PNC BANK ARTS CENTER

My second and final stop on the Oddball fest tour was in Holmdel, New Jersey, at the PNC Bank Arts Center, formerly the Garden State Arts Center and also the place where, in 1990, Sinéad O'Connor refused to go on when she found out the venue's policy of playing the national anthem before every show. They honored her request that they not play it, but Frank Sinatra was there the next night and said he wanted to "kick her in the ass."

This crowd was a bit larger than the one at Jones Beach, I'd say around fourteen thousand, so one of the biggest I'd ever played to. I went on first again and was having fun when a guy yelled from the back, "We can't hear you!" I was amused that he couldn't hear *me*, but somehow I could hear *him*, and I was speaking into a microphone that was blasting out of a giant PA system. This is not the first time I've encountered the "We can't hear you" thing. I usually try to nip it in the bud by talking to the sound person before shows and saying, "I'm really quiet, so please turn me up." I don't remember if I warned them before this show; I probably assumed that since it was an amphitheater, they could turn it up as loud as necessary.

Onstage at PNC Bank Arts Center. Holmdel, New Jersey.

After my fifteen-minute set, I walked out into the crowd, something I didn't do in Jones Beach. I like going out in big venues and seeing the show from the audience's perspective. I watch the comic onstage and think, *Ooh, that's what I do for a living!* It also gives the audience a chance to mob me for selfies. This didn't happen much when I went out there in New Jersey, but I ended up standing with Sal Vulcano from the TV show *Impractical Jokers*, who got asked multiple times for pictures. I was like, *Hell*-oh, *the dude wasn't even on the show tonight!*

After the show I was told we were getting a police escort out of the grounds. I got in the van with Michael Che, Jay Pharoah, and Anthony Jeselnik, pretty excited about this new, but long overdue, experience.

After driving about a half a minute, I realized there must have been several tiers of police escorts, and we got the *bronze* package. The police car just drove ahead of us until there was a clear path to drive out of there. It was like a twenty-foot police escort. I know it's weird to complain about a police escort, but that's what comedians do: complain about free hotels and police escorts. You might think a van full of comedians must be a nonstop laugh fest, but it wasn't. I mean, I imagine a witty comment was spoken, but the craziest thing that happened on this ride? Jay Pharoah blowing some vape smoke into my face on the trip home. I think it may have been an accident, and he eventually apologized. This story has a great ending: I accepted his apology!

THE IMPROV

There was a sixteen-year gap between my appearances at the Tempe Improv. I first worked there in 1999 when I co-headlined with the late Mitch Hedberg. *Co-headlining* is comedy booker shorthand for "We don't think you're ready to headline." On some level I understood the practice: they got two headliners for what they'd have to pay one, and you got to tell people you were sort of headlining. As a co-headliner, you performed for about forty minutes, but a conventional comedy club headlining set is forty-five minutes. So if you're a weak act who shouldn't be headlining, the audience still sees you for about the same amount of time, but I hadn't headlined much at that point, and Mitch was a great comic. (I saw him before he was famous when my manager took me to see him open for Ellen DeGeneres. Ellen's crowd wasn't really Mitch's *target audience*, but he held his ground and had a solid set under the circumstances.)

I flew with Mitch from New York. I had Gold status with Continental Airlines (it was still an airline at the time), which meant I had the chance to upgrade myself *and* a traveling companion if there was space available. We arrived at the airport. I told Mitch I might have a surprise for him. I whipped out the card. The gate agent poked around on her computer a bit, then ripped up our boarding passes and handed us new ones with first-class seats. I don't think the term "baller" existed back then, but that's what I felt like. I expected Mitch to be overwhelmed with joy and appreciation. Instead he fell asleep. He woke when we landed and muttered, "Thanks."

Mitch and I arrived in Tempe and stood at the front door of the *comedy condo* we were sharing. A comedy condo is a shitty apartment rented by the club because it's even cheaper than putting you up in a shitty hotel. Every club claims, "Our condo is actually good," but they're never good. Or they're good for the first two months, until the sofa in the living room accumulates its fiftieth ketchup stain (and that would be one of the better stains you'd find). Some comics like to cook on the road, so you would show up to the condo and find half a bag of hot dog buns tied with a twist tie sitting on the counter.

I stayed at an especially awful condo in Atlanta years ago. The funny thing is that the club had a deal with a limo company. So they'd pick you up at the airport and you'd arrive in what was a war zone of an apartment complex, but you'd be sitting in the back of a white stretch Cadillac.

There was supposed to be a key left for Mitch and me, but there wasn't and we couldn't get in. We called the owner and he said he'd just put us up in a hotel for the night. I thought, *Yeah, that's the way you handle that situation!* I imagined him telling us the next day, "Well, we got the condo door open, but I don't have the heart to move you from a nice hotel to our condo, so just stay there." But we just got one night at the hotel before moving into the modest two-bedroom condo. It wasn't too awful, but I remember getting mad at Mitch because he used my towel, which I guess was *our* towel.

There are a handful of comedy club owners who don't want male comics to *intermingle* with their female staff. This doesn't just mean dating and sex, this means *any* sort of contact outside of the club. I guess they think the $20 shift pay they give the waitresses entitles them to control their private lives. Well, the owner of this club was like that. I had a few nice chats with a woman who worked there, and when we met for an innocent burrito the next day, it was plotted like I was having an affair with the boss's wife. And the next day the owner was asking me what I did the previous night, and it was *so* obvious he was looking to "bust" me. It went something like this:

"So, Todd, what did you do yesterday?"

"Not much, just walked around, got some food."

Pause.

"Oh, just by yourself?"

"Pretty much."

I guess he was hoping I'd say, "Okay. You got me! I asked an adult to have lunch with me, and she said yes. She's an employee of yours and I know that's wrong. She won't be able to serve drinks later because she'll be too distracted by our burrito date. It won't happen again. I'm sorry."

I returned in 2015 for just one Friday-night show. In the sixteen years since I'd played the club, I had achieved the coveted "no condo" status, so I stayed at a good hotel.

I met up with my friend Chris Fairbanks, a funny LA comic I've known for many years, who was opening for me in Tempe, then Tucson and Missoula. He has a fun podcast he hosts with Karen Kilgariff called *Do You Need a Ride?* where they interview you while driving you somewhere. I've been on a few times, usually getting a ride from the Los Angeles airport. I love a free ride and Chris and Karen are fun to talk to, so everyone wins.

The Tempe Improv is a pretty massive club. Probably one of the biggest in the country. I didn't sell it out, but there were plenty of people there.

My brother lives in the area, so he came to the show with a bunch of his coworkers. The wrestler Dolph Ziggler was also there. I'd met him once and knew him a bit from Twitter. Yes, it's possible to know someone a bit from Twitter.

I hung out in the front bar after the show, and ate some sriracha chicken bites and both sweet potato and regular fries. I talked to Dolph (not his real name) a bit. He told me he was on the road 275 days a year. I like being on the road, but I think I'd go crazy doing it that much. Yes, the frequent-flier miles and hotel points would be nuts, but even I have my limits. Two hundred seventy-five days? That means you're only home three months of the year. I'm *so* glad I turned down that offer from the WWE in 1997.

A guy approached me at the bar and asked me, "So, what's your best joke ever?" I took a deep breath. The kind you take to avoid getting angry.

"I just did an hour of jokes. I'm a little fried," I said in my most accommodating voice.

"But really, what's like the best joke you've ever told?" he said, persisting.

I know I could've thought of a joke to tell him, but I'd just done an entire show. So I found another way of saying, "I don't think I'm up for that." He eventually walked away—and I'm sure told the people he was with that I'm an asshole. But I wanted to just chill with my brother, friends, and sriracha chicken bites! Also, he not only asked me to tell him a joke, it had to be my *best* joke? I don't spend a lot of time ranking my jokes in order of quality. I guess I could've said, "I love all my jokes equally. We'd be here for days if I rattled them all off. Please don't make me choose!" Actually, that's what I should have said.

CLUB CONGRESS

I drove to Tucson with Chris Fairbanks. He dropped me off at the Congress Hotel, home of Club Congress, a club I'd played three times since 2006. Up until my historic first visit, the hotel was known as the place where John Dillinger was caught in 1934.

It's a very unique, old hotel, with charming but smallish rooms that don't have a TV (although there's a giant flat-screen TV in the hallway), and there's a great restaurant and bar in the lobby.

It definitely has more character than a chain hotel, but it's also one of those hotels where you always think someone is opening your door. They still use actual keys instead of key cards, and there's no elevator. The first room they gave me was really small, so I asked for a new one. The second room was fine, but I noticed the window lock was broken. This wouldn't have been a problem, but directly outside the window—I mean inches away—was a bench. So someone could sit on this bench, casually open my window, and steal my collection of rubies and emeralds.

The last time I performed at Club Congress there was a woman in the audience who was a little chatty and rambunctious, who interrupted the show a few times. Afterward she did something that almost never happens: she apologized. She walked up and said something like "You're trying to do a show, you don't need someone like me getting in the way." Part of me wanted to say, "Too little, too late," but a bigger part of me gained some new faith in humanity.

This time there were some chatty people in the crowd, and after the show Chris told me he'd shushed them. I found out later that the people he shushed were on my guest list. A woman I'd met on a previous trip and her friends showed up a bit intoxicated. Nice people, but drunk and chatty. This is not the first time I've had problems with people I've invited. On two other occasions, I've had people *thrown out* who were on my guest list. One time it was a man and woman I met at a comedy club bar in Cleveland. The woman recognized me, so I thought it would be cool of me to say, "I'm actually doing a show here tonight. I could get you in." They ended up in the front row, where the guy proceeded to make phone calls during the show (to be fair, this was before texting, so he probably would've chosen that rude route if it happened today). So they got booted. Another time was in New York. A woman I barely knew asked if I could get her into another club I was working. I did, and she ended up *not agreeing* with Aziz Ansari's joke, so she started a midshow dialogue before I had her tossed.

I met up with my shushed friend and her shushed friends after. Like most people who get shushed, she didn't apologize, but I don't love confrontation (I know, everyone says that), so we went to a nearby bar that had pizza and sat around for a bit analyzing some text messages one of the women had received from some dude she was seeing. In one of them he texted back, "Well played," to something she'd sent, and I had to assure her this was a positive response.

I had the next day off, so I went to a coffee place that has several Arizona locations I've visited in the past. The coffee is always good. I walked up and looked at their specials board. They had a drink listed that I wasn't familiar with; I think it was some type of matcha drink.

"What's matcha?" I asked.

"You don't know what matcha is?" he asked, as if I were asking just to kill time.

"I really don't know what it is."

He then indulged me by explaining a drink that was on the menu of the coffee shop he chose to work at. Maybe I misread his tone, but he seemed like a bit of a worm. I fantasized about taking a picture of him and tweeting it to the coffee chain's account along with *This guy was very rude to me at your Tucson location*. But I didn't take a picture of him. And maybe he was a nice guy who didn't realize he came across like a shithead, or maybe he wasn't even a shithead. Story of my life. Always giving people the benefit of the doubt. *Sigh*.

I went for a walk on one of the main shopping streets, where I had my favorite moment of the trip. I passed by some sort of hippie supply store. A woman walking near me told her friend, "I want a pendulum, I just can't afford the one I want." Oh man, I get it, you don't want an *entry-level* pendulum. That was like the most *Tucson-y* thing I've ever heard, and if I'd walked by them five seconds earlier I would've missed it.

I ate two dinners that night, a burger at one restaurant, corn chowder at another. I walked by a place called Hub, which is like a lounge that sells ice cream. Sometimes you want to do the saddest thing possible on the road. So I went in there and had a little scoop of ice cream. All by myself. In a bar that also sold ice cream.

The next morning I wanted to meet up with my brother, who lived about ninety minutes away. The promoter was nice enough to give me a lift, but I think he was headed there anyway. I'm still counting that as a favor.

I spent the night at my brother's, then had my second-favorite moment of the trip. I was going through security at the Phoenix airport. There was a TSA agent who was trying way too hard to be funny. I don't remember what he said but it was on the level of saying, "Age before beauty," as people lined up. After a series of lame jokes, a dude in line looked at him and said, "You should try to get onstage at the Improv." Oh man. I enjoyed that.

STAGE 112

My first show in Missoula was a bit of a nightmare, but also a nightmare I look back at fondly. It was 2009, and I was booked at a place called the Palace with Chris Fairbanks opening for me. He's from Missoula, so he helped draw some people (or *put butts in seats*, as a club owner might say). We met up with the booker at a bar. He was amiable enough, but also seemed drunk every time I dealt with him. When I arrived at the venue, he escorted me to a cluttered storage closet to hang out in. It was so disgusting that even if I'd had a proper dressing room and walked by this makeshift one, I might have said, "Hey, you might want to tidy up your storage closet at some point." There was no food or drink put out, but it was littered with Taco Bell wrappers, as if to prove that someone at some point had actually eaten in there. I asked if I could get some water. It must have been the first time an artist had made such an unusual request, because they were not ready for it. The promoter scrambled around the club in search of this elusive *elixir*.

When he returned he said they didn't have any. No water? A bar with no water? And no stores nearby that sell it? At that point he held up the bottle of water *he'd* been drinking and said, "Want some?"

The crowd at the Palace was pretty rowdy, and this booker made the *executive decision* to let Chris Fairbanks do a lot of extra time. I like the comic on before me to do about fifteen to twenty minutes, mainly because I'm anxious to get onstage, and a short opening set makes it less likely the audience will get tired during my set. But Chris is a friend, and he was a local, so I didn't complain much.

Before the show some guy chatted with me near the bar. He was perfectly normal and coherent. I ran into him after the show and he was falling-down drunk. I wanted to ask, "How many drinks could you *possibly* have had in the hour I was onstage? I mean, did you do a shot every time you heard a perfectly crafted punch line?"

After the show, I met up with the booker to *settle up*, which is performer talk for "get paid." He handed me a wad of cash and a piece of paper with the number of people in attendance and my total pay scrawled on it. A better venue would have had a *settlement sheet* that was like a real spreadsheet: easy to read and everything itemized. I looked at the numbers on the scrap of paper, and based on the ticket price, there was no way his figures were accurate. I pointed this out to him and he said, "Oh yeah, some people showed up late, so I started *cutting deals*." He actually said "cutting deals." Like, "You missed the first five minutes of the show, so I'm gonna knock twenty percent off your admission fee! Prices are slashed!" I'm pretty sure my contract didn't have a "feel free to *cut deals*" clause.

I returned to Missoula in 2015. I arrived a day early and met up with Chris, who was opening for me again. While I was waiting for him in my hotel lobby, a very enthusiastic woman named Jackie approached. She said she was at the hotel with her improv troupe and they were doing a show for some electrical workers in one of the conference rooms later.

"Do you want to stop by?"

I'm not a huge improv fan, but if I had a choice between watching an improv troupe do a show in a Montana hotel conference room for electrical workers, and a lunch with the president at the White House, I would choose the improv show without even mulling it over. Yes, Jackie, I want to stop by.

Chris arrived, and I told him the good news. We walked around the hotel and found the conference room. As someone who has performed in his share of private shows in hotel conference rooms, I was prepared for an uncomfortable scene, like people talking, general conference room chaos. But we walked in to find the show in progress, and the improv troupe was killing. About forty rugged electrical workers (all men except for one woman) were scattered about in a room that probably held a hundred fifty, completely enraptured.

Chris and I headed out to get some food. I'd been told by multiple people to get a burger at the Missoula Club. Sometimes you ask ten people where to eat and you get ten different answers. Pretty much everyone I asked told me to get a burger at the Missoula Club. It was sort of a dive bar with pool tables, with a tiny grill. It seemed like the type of place where a lot of fights might break out but probably don't. But maybe they do. Whenever I go to a highly recommended restaurant, I wonder if I can judge the food fairly. Like when a bunch of people start talking about a band. I listen and go, "Oh yeah. I get it," even if I don't. But this burger was simple, good, and *unassailable*. And the brawl I got into was also wonderful!

The next day I grabbed lunch by myself at the Dinosaur Cafe. After I declined an offer for Creole mayonnaise for my po'boy, the manager walked by and said in an ominous voice, "No one refuses the Creole mayonnaise." His tone was playful—I felt no palpable sense that he would injure me if I didn't try a specialty mayonnaise—so I gave it a whirl. It tasted good, but part of me wished I'd held my ground and refused it, just to see if he actually would've killed me.

I often go online to see what other performers are in a town while I'm there. This time my only competition was a guy named Todd Snider, one of those names I see all the time but I have very little idea of what he does. What I do know is that he plays bigger places than I do. And I bet he's a nice guy. Another *Todd* example of this kind of artist is Big Head Todd and the Monsters. I see posters for them in half the cities I play. I know, we should all go on the road together.

My show at Stage 112 was way better than my previous one. Chris did have a moment where he had to tell his own friends to be quiet, but they settled down and were polite for me. And there was a dressing room. There was water in it. And as far as I know, no deals were *cut*.

SEPTEMBER 17, 2015—BOISE, IDAHO
LIQUID LAUGHS

first went to Boise in early 2000 to perform at the Funny Bone, a room that enjoyed an excellent reputation among comics. The owner had good taste in comedy and the room was well *policed* by the bouncers. It was the type of place where you would do your show and find out afterward that they threw six people out while you were up there, and you didn't even notice. They also had a great preshow announcement where they *congratulated* people who had cell phones before instructing them to turn them off. This was followed by my favorite line: "And please remember, when you're drinking, you think you're whispering, but you're not." Perfect.

It seemed like half the people I met in Boise were studying massage therapy. When I returned in 2002, I mentioned to the club manager that maybe I should get a massage while I was in town. He said he knew someone who would probably give me one in exchange for *free passes to the Funny Bone.* I'm sure my immediate reaction was "Why don't you just give her some passes? I bet there's a stack somewhere on top of your desk." Of course I didn't say that, so now I was faced with a dilemma: I wanted a free massage, but paying with comedy club passes felt wrong—embarrassing, actually. Scoring free passes from a chain comedy club is not exactly as challenging as scoring Radiohead tickets. Of course, I said yes, and the manager set it up. My guilt got worse when I realized she'd opened her studio to me on a Sunday, a day it was normally closed. The massage was good, but it was hard to relax knowing how I was going to pay for it. When she was done, I gave her a solid tip, but when I handed her that fistful of Funny Bone passes, yikes, I felt a little dirty.

The Funny Bone eventually moved to a different location, and when I returned in 2015 it had new owners and was now called Liquid Laughs.

I caught a 6:30 a.m. flight from Missoula, then checked into a place called the Modern Hotel, a former Travelodge that was redesigned as a hip boutique hotel. It violated my "No hotels where the doors open to the outside" rule, but it didn't violate my "I love boutique hotels" rule. And the thing with the door wasn't a big issue. I felt safe. Of course, I had to move rooms when the first one they gave me was next to the noisy and heavily trafficked housekeeping storage closet.

I did my usual coffee research and found a place called District Coffee. A lot of people think Boise is some backwoods place. I always tell them, "If I dropped you in Boise and told you it was Portland, Oregon, you wouldn't know the difference." Sweet people. Lots of tattoos. District Coffee could've been in Portland. They had a great sign near the counter that said "$1 credit card minimum." I don't know if that was a joke or they were really warding off people who tried to charge whatever they sold that was under a dollar. I hope it wasn't a joke.

Chris Fairbanks had to go back to LA after Missoula, so a local comic named Sean Peabody opened for me. He bills himself as "the Hawaiian Comedian." I didn't have a Hawaiian comedian open for me in Hawaii, but I had one in Idaho.

I went back to the Modern after the show and sat at the bar. It had a nice *mixology* vibe, but I didn't feel like drinking. I asked the bartender if he could make something "fun" that didn't have alcohol. He suggested a ginger limeade. Ginger and lime are two of my favorite flavors, so this was a mocktail *slam dunk*.

I had a day off between Boise and the next show, in Ogden, Utah. I chose to spend it in Boise. I roamed around a bit, stopped into a place called City Peanut Shop. I asked for something spicy. The nice man suggested a sample of their "ghost pepper" peanuts. I've watched the Travel Channel, so I knew the ghost pepper is extremely hot, but I still expected to go, "You call this spicy? That's adorable! This is like a *dessert* peanut." Ate a couple of them. Couldn't do it!

Went to District Coffee again. The walls of the restroom had a nice pattern, white, but with big black plus signs (I'm sure if the artist reads this, they'll say, "They weren't *plus signs*, you fucking idiot"). I loved the pattern, so I took a bathroom selfie that became the talk of Instagram for several weeks.

I stopped by Liquid Laughs that night just to see what was going on, and because comedy venues feel like a safe choice when I don't know what to do with myself. They had some local comics on. I watched a bit, then headed out for dinner.

Men's room. District Coffee, Boise, Idaho.

Someone recommended going to a Basque restaurant called Bar Gernika for my last meal. Boise has the largest concentration of Basque Americans in the country, so this seemed appropriate. I ordered chorizo and fries, not the healthiest choice, I know, but the one that showed the most respect to Basque and Idaho culture.

WISEGUYS

In 2010 a kind, optimistic promoter thought it would be a good idea to put me in a five-hundred-seat theater in Salt Lake City and pay me like it was sold out. About a hundred people showed up (I remember I got a good review of this show but was mad that the writer claimed I performed for "ninety minutes to fifty people" when it was more like sixty minutes to one hundred people.) It was a fun show, but the promoter lost some (probably a ton of) money. I hope I didn't discourage him from ever booking another comedian.

I returned in 2011 to a club called Wiseguys, which has a few locations in Utah. I was booked in the Salt Lake City suburb of West Valley. I blame the poor attendance for these shows on the fact that it was Thanksgiving weekend. You'd think maybe people would want to go out after being cooped up with their families, but I guess they wanted to continue hanging out with their families. Or maybe they didn't want to see me. But in the comedy world, it is considered to be a slow weekend.

I remember a couple came into the club—I assume they were Mormons—and inquired if the show was dirty. The woman at the ticket window couldn't really give a specific answer—that's kind of a hard question since you don't know what will offend someone, and she may not have been familiar with my act—so the couple took a chance. I glanced at them while I was onstage, and they were laughing throughout the show. Afterward they approached me and said they'd had a great time. I respected that they asked about the content in advance, rather than showing up, getting offended, and then sending an angry e-mail to the club. I once opened for Ricky Gervais at the beautiful Chicago Theatre. I was in the lobby after the show and witnessed a woman ask for a *comment card* because she was offended by Ricky's antireligion material. If she'd done her research, that wouldn't have happened. Also, what would filling out a comment card accomplish? He sold ten thousand tickets over two nights. Did she think the promoter would ask for his money back?

I'd heard good things about the Ogden location of Wiseguys for years, so I had my agent book me there in 2015.

I announced the show on Twitter and a guy responded: *Got all excited seeing that @toddbarry is coming back to UT. Then realized Wiseguys is sticking him in Ogden. Super weak.* I fired back with: *I asked to go there.* Then the guy responded with, *I can respect that. If Ogden is to have a show, who better than the World's Most Adorable Comedian? Just wish I could make it!* "Adorable," huh? Better than being "super weak." Good response.

I had a distorted preconception of Ogden. I expected a sparse suburb off a big highway, like one of those places that has a weird pocket of hotels where there's a Courtyard by Marriott right next to a Residence Inn by Marriott. (If you are a Marriott Rewards member you are slapping your knees now.)

Ogden turned out to be a real city. I know I sound awful saying that, but you know what I mean.

I was given a suite at the Hampton Inn that was bigger than my apartment in New York. I walked through the hall and heard very loud dance music blasting from one of the rooms. The door was open and I saw a housekeeper working to the beat. The volume was so beyond acceptable that I could only be happy for her.

I took a longish walk to a coffee shop I'd read about, only to find that it was just a takeout place. I used to like walking around with a coffee, then I discovered the joy of sitting in a coffee shop staring into space while taking an occasional break to do some work. Since I was there I ordered an iced coffee. Right across the street was Lee's Mongolian BBQ. I love Mongolian barbecues. I like that you get to control what you're eating. This place had good reviews and it was right there, so I went in with a close-to-full iced coffee in my hand. Now, when I see someone bring in a drink to a restaurant, I get very self-righteous. *Maybe the people in the FOOD AND DRINK business don't want you to bring in your own FOOD OR DRINK.* But I felt like I could be forgiven because of the no-seats situation at the coffee shop. Was I supposed to stand outside while I finished a sixteen-ounce iced coffee? I hid the cup on the seat of the booth, so it was less tacky, then I got in line. A delightful man, who I believe was Lee, welcomed me. He asked me if I'd had Mongolian barbecue before and was there to help me assemble the perfect bowl of food. A Mongolian barbecue is a great place to see gluttony at its best. People stuff so much food into the bowl that it makes me embarrassed to be in the same restaurant. I stuffed a *respectable* amount of food into mine, added a *secret combination* of sauces that I'll never reveal under any circumstances, then sat down. The waitress brought over a basket of bread, which seemed weird and inauthentic. But I've never been to Mongolia, so maybe putting bread out lets you know you're at the *real deal*.

I left Lee's and stopped in a Mexican candy shop. I gotta buy Mexican candy! I'm in Ogden, Utah! I bought a couple of bags of a fruit candy that was spiked with chili pepper. How often do you see that? I was excited as I walked back to the hotel with this unusual purchase. Then I tripped on an uneven part of the sidewalk. As I hit the concrete the candy went flying. Each piece was individually wrapped, so I guess it would've been safe to gather some up and bring it home, but I was angry and humiliated, and my hands were scraped. I didn't want candy that had been on the sidewalk, even if it was wrapped. So I gathered up the spilled candy and heaved the bag into a garbage can. I walked back feeling like a ten-year-old boy who'd dropped his lunch box.

I walked into the Harvest Moon Celebration, a street fair with bands playing. A sign at the entrance said "No Outside Food." That's hard-core for a street fair. I bought a sweet "Ogden, Utah" T-shirt, which I wear quite a bit.

A capacity crowd was waiting for me at the club. In the middle of the show I noticed a guy taping me and made him turn it off. He later explained that he'd driven three hours to see me. That was nice to hear, but I still didn't want him taping me. I don't think he was trying to guilt-trip me. If I did, I would've told him how I once drove twelve hours to see REM in Atlanta. I didn't tape them.

I was hungry after the show, so someone from the club took me to a pizza place called Lucky Slice. I got a pepperoni slice that was so delicious, I added Ogden, Utah, to the list of places you might not think have good pizza but do. Right after Durham, North Carolina.

When I got back to New York, I looked for my check and realized it had been in an envelope with another piece of paper I didn't need, so I'd ripped it up. I wouldn't describe myself as *flaky*—I know people who forget to deposit their paychecks—so I felt angry in that way that makes you say "I don't make mistakes like this! I love doing comedy, and I'd do it for free, but if you give me a check, I will most likely cash it."

THE BARTLETT

I was at a They Might Be Giants concert many years ago in Central Park. I was in the fenced-off VIP area, just watching the show like everyone else, but later someone posted on an Internet message board that I was standing there in a way that said, "Look, everyone, I'm Todd Barry." I sort of know what that look is (because I do it now on purpose) but I also think she was projecting it on me: she didn't like me, so she came up with the worst interpretation of how I stood at a concert. I doubt I was standing there pointing to myself, hoping to upstage a band that was playing for five thousand people.

I bring that up because on my way to Spokane, I spotted Geraldo Rivera at LaGuardia Airport, and I wondered if he was doing what I was accused of. He walked by me while I was waiting at my gate, alone and not wearing a hat. As far as celebrity sightings go, this was a *direct hit*. He sat down, but then he kept getting up to run mysterious errands. One time he came back with some food, but there was no explanation for the other times. Maybe he was thinking, *I'll do one more lap and someone will approach me.* But no one did, and it inspired me to tweet this:

At LaGuardia airport having a "not getting recognized" contest with Geraldo Rivera.

I should've tagged him in the tweet. Maybe he would've found me and said, "What is *with* these people? Don't they know who *we* are?"

I got to Spokane the day before the show. The shower was clogged at my hotel. I'd say this happens at half the hotels I stay at. Sometimes it's just a matter of figuring out how to open the drain, but not in this case. It was my first shower there, so my awful, hairy apelike body couldn't be blamed.

At this point you're thinking, *Todd, did you plan your Spokane trip to coincide with the Washington State Chinese Lantern Festival that was going on at the time?* I did not. It was a wonderful co-incidence. I asked someone what I should do that night, and they suggested checking out the festival. I'd never heard of such a thing, and thought I might not ever hear of such a thing again, so I figured that was the place to go. I was hungry, so I was excited to eat some great Chinese food while checking out some sweet Chinese lanterns. By the time I got there, they'd stopped serving the authentic Chinese food, so all that was left was typical festival fare like kettle corn and pizza. I love both those things, but they didn't seem to fit into the culinary vibe I was trying to create for myself. I enjoyed look-ing at the various lanterns, but all the colorful illuminated zebras, butterflies, peacocks, elephants, and giraffes triggered my somewhat compulsive picture taking. I grabbed many shots, including some of my famous selfies. Even if you're antiselfie, you won't be at a Chi-nese lantern festival.

Chinese Lantern Festival. Spokane, Washington.

I spent an hour walking around the festival. I caught a few minutes of—and took a few pictures of—a dance troupe performing on one of the outdoor stages, before I left to get some food at a sleek ramen place called Nudo. After dinner I found a bar called Volstead Act that was quiet until some loudmouthed guy whom I dubbed "the Ernest Hemingway of Spokane" showed up and started yelling (to be fair, I have no idea if Hemingway was a loudmouth). I'm guessing he was a *regular* because the bartender *tolerated* him. I hate loudmouths at bars as much as I hate couples who make out at bars. I remember going to a bar in the East Village in New York City. A couple started making out inches from me. I made a face and the bartender, who I was friendly with, walked over to them and said, "We're closing up." I appreciated that.

I got a message from my comedian friend David Angelo, who said he'd be in Spokane the next day to open for John Mulaney.

David was staying across the street at the same hotel as Def Leppard. I knew they were in town, and there were tour buses parked out front, so I assume it was them, and not David's busses. He walked over to my hotel lobby, but somehow neither of us realized the other one had arrived. David asked the doorman to call me, and he whispered I was sitting in the corner. Later on David claimed I was "hiding" in the corner, but that sounds dramatic.

We got lunch at a place called Neato Burrito, then went to get a coffee at a shop that also sold home goods.

While checking out the bathroom supplies, David made the bombshell comment that you can't get a good soap dish.

I pursued this topic with the same fervor with which most people would avoid it.

"What do you mean, David?" I could feel myself getting upset.

"They don't have any drainage. The soap just sits in a puddle of water."

"I don't know, David. I feel like I've seen a soap dish that drains. I bet I even OWN one."

"They don't make one that drains."

"It's 2015. I'm pretty sure they've nailed down soap dish design."

David held his ground: they just don't make soap dishes correctly. For some people it would've been the perfect time to change the subject, but since there were a Macy's, Pottery Barn, and Anthropologie within walking distance, changing the subject didn't seem appropriate. Proving my point did. I was nice enough to explain to the polite saleswoman at Anthropologie the big feud we were having. She was patient and I felt bad for dragging her into my silliness. David rejected all the soap dishes she showed us, so I decided to let it go. I should point out that months earlier, David had started a company that sold

old-fashioned double-edged safety razors. He sent me one, and I was never able to shave in under twenty minutes. So maybe he's not one to talk about bathroom product design.

The show that night was at the Bartlett, a relatively new music venue. It only held one hundred for a seated show, so it was an easy sellout, and the place was well run and clean.

Front door. The Bartlett. Spokane, Washington.

I talked to a guy during the show who worked at a place called Papa Murphy's Take N' Bake Pizza, a chain I'd never heard of but is apparently quite popular in the area. He revealed that Papa Murphy's sells *uncooked* pizzas.

"Like you order a pizza just how you like it, then you take it home and *bake it yourself*?"

The audience was delighted at how delighted I was about the concept, but I felt uneasy pursuing it too much because I'm guessing it was probably something everyone in the crowd had made fun of at some time. Like how some American comics do shows in England and talk about how the police there don't use guns. It's too obvious. I'm supposed to be funnier than the audience.

There were limited after-show food options, so I met up with David Angelo for my second Neato Burrito meal of the day. There was an open mic going on, and it felt weird standing in a burrito line while a comic was onstage ten feet from me. The audience was shitty and talkative, so I ate my food and went back to Volstead Act. Pretty good two days in Spokane. My first Chinese lantern festival and an extended conversation about soap dishes.

THE WILD BUFFALO

I have a financial application on my computer called Quicken, which I use to track my income and expenses. (Please don't stop reading. There's a reason I brought this up.) Quicken comes in handy during tax time, but it's also good for research, like if someone tweets to me, *How come you never come to Chicago?* I can do a search and write back, *Well, actually, I've done* nine *shows in Chicago in the past two years.* I started using the software in 1999, so I can't research shows I did before then, like my first one in Bellingham, Washington. I do remember it was at a restaurant and pub called Elephant & Castle. I walked into the place and immediately sized it up as a bad gig about to happen. There was a large bar off to the side (where I thought people would get chatty) and a significant number of people seated behind the stage. Big bar, behind-stage seats: I was prepared for a disaster. To my surprise, the people sitting behind the stage stopped talking and behaved like they had good seats. Same with the bar. I love when my preconceptions about a show are wrong. It happens a lot. I'll hear people talking as they walk into the club, one of them will say something stupid like "We should heckle," and I assume they're going to ruin the show. Then the lights come down and they're little angels!

I arrived for a sound check and found the dressing room empty, as in no food or drink. The promoter running the show said he hadn't looked at my rider (even though it was already seven thirty). He was apologetic and got me some food and water. Shortly after that he walked in and said that he felt bad about not being prepared, so he would adjust the deal so I'd get 100 percent of the ticket sales after expenses. Apology accepted.

I heard the sound of a flute emanating from somewhere backstage. *Why am I hearing a flute backstage at my comedy show?* It wasn't a recorded flute. It's not like the dishwasher was listening to *flute music* while working. This was a *live* flute. I walked around the various rooms in the basement and found an older long-haired dude just sitting in a chair playing a flute. I'm hypersensitive to noise (as you know) and have knocked on the doors of noisy neighbors before, like the young guitarist who lived above me in my first East Village building. He was playing—and I'm not lying—"Stairway to Heaven" accompanied by a keyboardist in his apartment above me. I walked upstairs and pounded on his door. I don't really enjoy confrontations, so I was proud of myself for the force of my door pounding. This wimpy, terrified kid opened the door, looking like the least-manly guy at Best Buy.

"Yeah, you can't play your music here," I said, all macho and tough.

"Oh, I thought it was during the day, so there wouldn't be anyone around."

"You didn't think anyone would be around during the day?"

He thought he had an *entire* New York City apartment building to himself because it was daytime (and this was in the East Village, a neighborhood full of people who don't work nine to five). Also, he was too young to be playing "Stairway to Heaven."

I didn't want to treat this old flautist as rough as my former neighbor, but his playing was loud, and I knew it would drive me nuts. So rather than confronting him myself, I had someone from the club do it. They said they knew the guy, which was disappointing. It would've been more fun if a guy just broke into the club to practice his flute.

Brendan Kelley was my opening act there and in Spokane. The promoter booked a local emcee, but then came in and told me there was a fourth act on the show. "Why is there a fourth act on the show?" I have a clause in my contract that forbids adding any acts to my shows without my approval (that's right, *forbids*!). This prevents what's known in the industry as a "guest set." A guest set is a short set by a comic who isn't on the show, usually about eight to ten minutes. Sometimes it's a local, sometimes it's a comic who is in town and wants to *jump onstage* while they're in the area. I did a club in DC once that put two guest sets on, at least one of whom was so terrible, they actually apologized after.

I don't like guest sets because there's nothing in it for me. I heard Chris Rock say the show should be a *setup* for the headliner, and I agree. If I let a guy do a guest set and he does a five-minute bit about Cheetos, and it turns out that's my closing bit, then I'm in trouble. The Cheetos bit wouldn't have the same *sting*.

But the fourth act ended up on this show due to unprecedented circumstances. The guy who was scheduled didn't want to emcee, so he just asked another comic to do it. I was stunned. "You just added someone to *my* show? I didn't know you were allowed to do that." It turned out I knew the fourth comic, a guy named Randall who appeared in the Vancouver segment of my special *The Crowd Work Tour*. I didn't have the strength to argue, and I didn't want to pull this guy from the show after he had appeared on my special, so I accepted it.

Brendan's parents lived nearby and were at the show. When this happens, I always like to start the show with something like "Let's hear it for Brendan Kelley. His *parents* are here. Let them know he made the right career choice!"

After the show I was standing by the merch table. A woman who looked a bit disturbed mumbled something weird, then walked off like I'd snubbed her. After the show Brendan and I were walking to a bar around the corner and I spotted a woman lying on her back on the sidewalk with her bag next to her. I said to Brendan, "I think that's the woman from the show." I walked over and found it was. I'd seen her slam a drink before she left the club and guessed she'd continued drinking at the nearby bar. A few random people were staring, but no one seemed overly concerned. I called 911 and then got someone from the club to check out the scene. Two cops showed up and tried hard to get her to stand up. She was resistant and cursing at them, but they remained calm, compassionate, and respectful. I'm guessing she had a lot to drink and perhaps some mental issues. I knew she was in good hands with these two cops, but I wanted to stick around for a bit: the situation was extra sad because she was at my show. I waited a good twenty minutes to see how it panned out. She hadn't gotten up but it was clear the cops weren't going anywhere. One of them said something like "We can't force you to get up, but we'd like to help you." Before I left, a guy standing by us thought it would be appropriate to quote one of my old jokes to me and compliment me on an appearance on an Adult Swim cartoon. I like compliments, but this seemed thoughtless. I gave him the smallest acknowledgment possible, then muttered to Brendan, "This guy's fucking unbearable."

On my flight home the woman seated in the window seat next to me warned me she'd be "getting up a lot." *Todd, how many times did she get up during the five-hour flight from Seattle?* The answer may surprise you: zero. Nice failed passive-aggressive attempt at snagging my aisle seat.

OCTOBER 14, 2015—OAKLAND, CALIFORNIA

THE PARISH

I flew to Oakland from Los Angeles. Things got off to a *terrible* start at LAX when I ordered a bagel and it was toasted in a panini press. I can't defend why that bothered me, but I bet they can't defend why they toasted a bagel in a panini press.

I'm actually not really that petty. For an airport bagel, it did the job. And those panini ridges did create a bagel texture sensation I only experience when I get a bagel at an airport. I followed this up with a banana peanut butter smoothie from Pinkberry, served to me by a woman who made great eye contact.

This was my first show ever in Oakland, although I think I've done more shows in nearby San Francisco than any other city outside of New York.

I took a Lyft from the airport, then got to my hotel and realized I'd undertipped the driver. *Todd, you accidentally undertipped someone? You've established that you're a great guy, so this must have tortured you*. It did. I tried to figure how to change my tip but couldn't. I know a guy who works for Lyft so I wrote to him and asked if there was a way to update my gratuity. After saying, *That's really nice of you*, he explained how to do it. I wrote back, *Great. That was easy. Thanks.* What I should've written back was *Yes, that* was *nice of me. Thanks.*

I couldn't find a decent hotel in Oakland, so I booked one in Berkeley, and when I got there I kind of wished I was doing a show in Berkeley, a vibrant college town filled with smart people who don't seem like jerks. I once met a woman who got her degree in *rhetoric* at Berkeley. I'd never heard of that major before. Now whenever I meet someone who went there I say, "Oh, were you a rhetoric major?" This causes them to faint, or at the very least cry tears of joy at my *inner sanctum* knowledge of their school.

I arrived at the Parish, a two-hundred-fifty-seat venue with a balcony. The guys who greeted me were friendly but seemed a bit unprepared for my arrival. We did a sound check, then they stuck me in an upstairs dressing room that was missing water, food, and toilet paper. I could probably hunt down my own water, but I wasn't going on a toilet paper run. I told one of the production guys about the unstocked dressing room. He asked what I wanted. Rather than telling them my minimal requirements, I got a little *hardball* and said, "It's all in my contract. You can just go look at it," knowing full well they hadn't read it. The guy left for a few minutes, then came back flustered and said, "Why don't you just tell us what you want. We'll get it for you." They also handed me a walkie-talkie to use when I wanted to start the show. This was a first, and it made me feel isolated and slightly panicky.

My opening act was Sean Keane, a smart, funny guy who often

opens for me when I'm in the Bay Area. When he arrived at the club he said to the doorman, "I'm here to open for Todd." The guy responded, "Who's Todd?" Nice, they didn't even know the name of that night's entertainment. That's like being a waiter and not knowing what the soup of the day is. *Todd, your "soup of the day" analogy really helped bring that point home!*

A comic named Christopher John had written to me and asked if he could do a guest set. Chris is featured in the opening shot of my special *The Crowd Work Tour*. When I talked to him for the special, I had no idea he was a comic. He sat in one of the first few rows, and comics are usually in the back. We had a funny exchange about the dog collar company he worked for. He really rode the line between seeming like he wanted to talk and being slightly shy. I wasn't familiar with his comedy but took a chance. He went up and did a series of filthy and hilarious one-liners. All comedians love filthy humor, even ones who don't work *blue*.

The show was packed and it made me forget the little complaints I had about the hospitality. Everyone was well behaved, but I did notice one woman who seemed like she was *on the verge* of yelling something out. I kept talking and at some point she yelled out, "Crowd work!"— referring to my special *The Crowd Work Tour*. This was not billed as a "crowd work" show, so I was irritated by her interruption. I explained that I preferred to do what I wanted onstage, rather than putting it out to *the people*. She calmed down, and the next day I got an e-mail from her husband apologizing for her behavior, saying, *She prefers your crowd work, and passion clouded her judgment when she drank an entire bottle of wine.* I prefer to think it wasn't the wine that caused her to speak up. I'd like to think it was the passion.

THE PUNCH LINE

There are two Punch Line comedy clubs in California. One is located across the hall from a mattress shop in a nondescript shopping center in Sacramento. I've worked the other location, in San Francisco, many times; they were one of the first clubs to headline me. But I hadn't been to the Sacramento club since 2003.

I returned to Sacramento in 2014 to the Comedy Spot, mainly an improv and sketch theater that dabbled in standup. The shows were great, but the thing that stood out was the booker handed me my check in the car on the way to the first show. That does not happen often. I went ahead and did the shows, even though I could have easily skipped town.

Sacramento has many Mongolian barbecue restaurants and I thought that was where I'd first eat at one on the tour. The one I randomly discovered in Ogden, Utah, was a real *outlier, shocker, aberration, and surprise.*

I did some research and found a place called Li's in the suburb of Carmichael, and drove over there with Sean Keane. We got in line, stuffed our bowls, then walked up to the sauce station, where all the *magic* happens at a Mongolian barbecue. They had the usual selection of sauces, like teriyaki, sesame, lemon, ginger, and garlic, but they had a sign suggesting adding one ladle of each kind of sauce to your bowl. This seemed rigid, almost like a *recipe*. I know the suggestion came from an actual chef, but you gotta let me *cut loose*, make some mistakes, some discoveries. Maybe I want to go *half* a ladle of garlic, but a *double* ladle of sesame. That sign is the *enemy of finesse*.

I had a wonderful experience in the elevator back at the Sacramento Hilton. The doors opened and a dude walked out holding a cat and a litter box. Nothing upstages a cat on an elevator like a litter box in the owner's other hand. I love cats and comedy, so I was delighted. I didn't even know you could travel with a cat. I guess you can, if you also travel with a litter box.

The show was not sold out, but a very *respectable* number of people showed up for a Thursday, and they were all warm. Afterward, I stood in the hall selling posters and taking pictures. One guy asked me to step away from the table, then walk twenty feet so we could pose in front of the mattress shop sign, probably because, like every comic who works there, I mentioned onstage that I was performing next door to a mattress shop. I told him I'd rather just take the picture right where we were. His date gave him a little shit for the request. I don't mind taking pictures—it's a quick transaction with a definite ending—but some people have a little theme with their pictures, like "I collect pictures of celebrities giving me the finger." *That sounds great. You won't be getting anything new for your collection tonight.* People also do things like that when they ask me to sign stuff. "Can you write, 'To Bob, I hope you die, you fucking piece of shit'?" *I'm just going to write, "Hi, Bob!"*

It was still early when the show ended. I had asked the audience, "Where's the after-show party?" A woman at the merch table mentioned a place called the Back Door Lounge. Sean and I drove to the hard-to-find bar. It had a lot going for it: neighborhoody retro vibe, not too crowded, friendly bartender, and Tom Petty playing over the sound system. The only thing missing was food, so we walked over to a great late-night Thai place called Thai Canteen. They had the typical spice-level choices—mild, medium, and hot—but they also had a level called "Thai hot." "What happens if I order Thai hot?" I asked the guy behind the counter.

"You die," he answered.

"I'll guess we'll go with hot."

I had the next day off, so I went to a great coffee shop called Insight. I'd discovered one of their other locations on my last trip to Sacramento.

I had this idea that Sean and I should go there to write. We brought our laptops and worked for a bit. I got hungry and a barista was nice enough to make a list of restaurants. We went to a place called Jacks Urban Eats, then stopped to buy something at Safeway, which had a large chrome statue of a horse out front. Yes, I took a picture. Later I read the statue is made of recycled car bumpers and is one of those polarizing pieces of public art. Some people love it, others don't. Whenever I read about a piece of public art that's upsetting people, I always take the side of the artist, even if I don't like the art. But I liked the giant chrome horse out front, so if I ever move to Sacramento, you know where I'm shopping.

Silver horse statue. Sacramento, California.

THE HOLLAND PROJECT

If someone tells me a city is "boring" it makes me want to go there and see for myself. A few people over the years have told me Reno is boring, but as soon as I arrived I realized they were wrong. How can you describe a city as "boring" when, on a Saturday night, you have your choice of seeing Mike Tyson's one-man show at a casino or Todd Barry doing comedy in a ninety-nine-seat all-ages performance space run by a nonprofit?

Yes, Mike Tyson was my competition in Reno. He was performing (if that's what you call it) at the casino hotel where I was staying. My show was sold out, so I'm sure his was empty. I'm joking. I bet Mike did fine. I can't imagine there were many people in Reno holding a quarter going, "Heads we see Barry, tails it's Tyson."

Sean Keane and I arrived at the Holland Project and were greeted by Britt, the director of the nonprofit, and Chris, the sound guy. The venue had a punk rock/art gallery vibe. It was packed with chairs and seemed like a great place for an intimate show.

There wasn't a proper dressing room, so they curtained off an area behind the stage, which had a table with a good spread of food and drinks. It was in the front of the venue, exposed to the street by a big window. I told Britt I felt weird being on display before the show, not really expecting a solution to this. She stepped in the back and returned with big rolls of brown paper—the kind they put up when a store goes out of business—which she cut and taped to the front window. It's like she was ready for this situation. I was the first comedian to perform there, and I can't imagine the thrash bands they usually book having this issue.

The show was sold out, but Britt asked if I wanted to offer some standing-room tickets. I said sure. Standing at a comedy show isn't ideal, but it's better (I think) than missing my amazing show.

Chris stepped outside for a bit. When he returned he told me, "There are some people outside who want to interview you for their podcast."

"Oh, I already told them I'm not up for that."

He went back outside and told them I didn't want to do it. He came back inside and said, "They said they still might ask you again."

Before I arrived in Reno, I'd gotten an e-mail from my manager's assistant telling me some college kids wanted me to do their podcast while I was in town. I don't love being interviewed, and I hate planning anything for my free time on the road, so I passed on a polite no. This wasn't acceptable to them, so now I had to deal with a second request and a warning to me that there would be a third request.

Before the show I got a text from my friend Joe Plummer, who has played drums with Modest Mouse and the Shins, and was now on tour with the Cold War Kids. They had an outdoor show scheduled in Reno that was canceled due to weather, so they were stuck in town with nothing to do. I put them on my guest list.

There was an interesting mix of people at the show, including a dude sitting up front with his parents and a musician who explained to me that "sex comcs from songs."

I didn't see Joe Plummer in the crowd when I was onstage, and I didn't see him after. A huge pet peeve for me is when people ask to be on my guest list, then don't show up. This happened to me in Athens, Georgia. A woman I knew asked to be on the list. She didn't show up. Later I received an apology Facebook message from her explaining she was at dinner with her friends and didn't get to the club until ten (when she thought I was going on), only to find out I'd already been on thirty minutes. She ended with my least-favorite phrase to see in an apology: *Don't hate me.* She also didn't explain why she didn't stay to watch the second half of my set, especially since she wasn't paying.

I looked for Joe after the show, then sent him this charming text: *Changed your mind about coming to my show?* It turns out he and his bandmate were outside saying good-bye to their two guests, one of whom had passed out during my set.

I was at the merch table when a bearded dude and a woman approached. I knew what was coming. "We do a podcast and wanted to see if we could interview you."

"Yeah, I heard. I'm sorry. I'm not really up for it. I just did an hour show and just want to relax."

So now I've said no to them three times.

"What are you doing tomorrow?" he continued.

"I'm leaving town."

I knew he wasn't done.

"What time is your flight?"

"Uh, one p.m."

He responded, "Oh!" like we'd figured out how to make this work.

"I can't do your podcast in the morning."

He and his crew nodded and slumped away. Yeah, let me *wake up early* to do your podcast *before I go to the airport.* Who wouldn't want to do that? See if Mike Tyson will do it, and don't take his first four no's as an answer.

Based on their massive sense of entitlement and pushiness, I knew that I'd hear from them again. A few days later some nasty tweets were directed at me from their podcast's account. One said, . . . *Bought standing room only tickets, got snubbed for a short interview. #ToddBarrySucks #FuckToddBarry*

This is not the first time I've been accused of "snubbing" someone. Someone in Nashville posted on Reddit once how I "snubbed" them after a show because I wanted to "chase skank ass." I wanted to respond, "Seems like I missed a great opportunity to hang out with someone who refers to women as 'skank ass.' Also the woman you were referring to was a platonic friend of mine of fifteen years who was from Nashville and back for a visit. And I talked to anyone from the audience who wanted to chat. So unless we had plans, I didn't snub you."

I like to take the high road in these situations, so I didn't respond to the tweet, but I like that they pointed out they bought standing-room tickets, as if *big fans buy standing-room tickets.* They bought standing-room tickets because they waited until the last minute. The people who were most excited to see me already had seats.

I met up with Sean, Joe, and his bandmate Matt at the 40 Mile Saloon. Britt was there with a cool young woman named Sophia who worked the show at the Holland Project. The bar didn't serve food, so Sophia walked me to a sports bar called Coach's that was open. It turned out Coach's was one of the few bars in Reno where you could still smoke. I'm used to bars and restaurants being smoke-free, but every couple of years I discover a pocket of the country where it's still allowed, and it seems nuts. I want to yell, "Do you see what's going on here? Someone call the cops!" I don't think Sophia's job description included exposing herself to sports bar smoke, but she was nice enough to run into the place and order my chicken fingers while I stood outside.

We took the food and went back to the 40 Mile Saloon, where I was awesome enough to share my fries with all takers. The next stop was a karaoke bar called the Point, where about twenty people were gathered, including a man in a sharp suit who seemed like a regular. I assume someone is a regular at a karaoke bar if they *bring their own microphone*. It's like guys who bring their own cues to pool halls. They're at a different level. And it wasn't just a microphone, it was a headset microphone, the favorite of stage hypnotists and TED talks. But nothing about this guy was pretentious or affected.

After a few young folks went up and sang some typical karaoke fare, it was time for the real deal. The man in the suit hopped on the tiny stage and sang an R & B song; it might have been a soul song. And when he sang, I realized this guy deserved to bring his own mic. He sang so well, and performed with such confidence, it was easy to imagine him onstage in front of two thousand people.

The next morning Sophia picked me up and took me to the Reno airport, which I found out is the closest airport to the Burning Man festival and even features a Burning Man museum. I've never been to Burning Man, and will never go, and I don't actually know what goes on there (even though I've asked ten people over the years), but I will explore a Burning Man museum, especially if it's in an airport. I checked out a few photographs. I still don't know what goes on there.

I took some pictures of the airport and was headed for security when it hit me. Something was missing. My backpack and laptop. I'm not a screamer or a yeller, which is bad when you have a legitimate reason to scream or yell. I ran toward the ticketing area, looked around, and then ran in a few random directions, aware that running around an airport is suspicious behavior. I went to the counter where I'd checked in. No one had turned in a backpack. She told me to call the lost and found. They didn't have it. I was on my way to my first public meltdown when I thought to call Sophia.

"Did I leave my backpack in the van?"

Brief pause. "Yes, you did!"

She drove back and handed me the bright blue bag.

I spent the rest of the trip making sure I hung on to that moment of relief. *Everything you care about is on that laptop. Pictures. Blackmail-ready e-mails. Video clips of you on* Letterman. *Think of all the great tweets that were written on that baby. Imagine how terrible you'd feel if you didn't get it back. But you did.* I celebrated with a nine-dollar airport pizza, then got the ultimate reward when I landed at gate 37 in Denver. My connecting flight left from gate 36.

NOVEMBER 5, 2015—JERSEY CITY, NEW JERSEY
MONTY HALL

The last time I had done a show in Jersey City was in 2013, and I was flat-out ripped off by the booker. It was a guy who had booked me in the past and paid me fine, so I didn't hesitate to work with him again. The show was at an Italian restaurant on the water. A bit hard to find, and not at all a place where you'd go, "*This* would be the *ideal* venue for a comedy show."

The restaurant gave me a great thin-crust pizza before the show, and the dressing room bathroom had the biggest bottle of hand soap I'd ever seen, so I felt fine about performing for the fifteen or so people, including my punk rock bass-player friend Jason Narducy. I've done thousands of shows for small crowds, so I went up and gave this little scattered gang a professional hour. Yes, I mentioned the size of the crowd a few times, but I didn't make them feel bad for showing up.

After the show we went backstage to get paid. The booker stepped out of the restaurant office looking sweaty and agitated.

"So, Todd, I'm having a problem here, can I get you the money tomorrow?"

Comedians generally get paid right after their shows unless other arrangements are made. Aside from traveling and making people laugh, a small joy of my job is getting paid right after I work; sometimes I'll use my Chase phone app to deposit my check backstage. I like getting paid on time, and for that reason, I pay people on time. My credit rating can only be described as *phenomenal*, and the last time I checked my PayPal payer rating it was like "A++++," and at least two of my Airbnb guest reviews point out that I'm "tidy." So when I hear "Can I pay you tomorrow?" my "about to get ripped off" radar starts beeping.

"Actually, I need to get paid tonight."

He huffed and puffed, then I suggested that he get my money at an ATM. He went away for a long time, then came back with a fistful of cash that was the amount I was paying my opener.

"Give that money to Doogie," I said. Doogie Horner had opened for me, and I didn't want him to get dragged into this mess.

The booker went on a few more mysterious trips but came back empty-handed, and I saw he was in a panic. I guess the person who owned the venue wasn't happy with the show and didn't want to give him the money he was supposed to give me. But I did the show and was entitled to get paid.

He pleaded with me to let him pay me the next day. The restaurant was about to close, and I wanted to get out of there, so I made him send me an e-mail declaring he owed me the money and that he would pay me the next day.

He didn't end up paying me the next day. He still hasn't paid me. It's been years. After many e-mails and calls from my agent (which he responded to with long, sweaty apologies, explanations of how broke he was, and declarations that paying me was a priority) he eventually sent me 12.5 percent of what he owed me. I could tell you the amount, but that would be tacky. (Hopefully he didn't pay me right after this book went to press; I wouldn't want to order a *massive recall*.)

I had no worries about getting ripped off when I returned to Jersey City in 2015. I was booked by a guy named Todd Abramson, who used to book a great Hoboken rock club called Maxwell's. I'd worked for him many times, and he's what's known in the business as a *straight shooter*. The show was at a venue with a funny name (Monty Hall) run by WFMU, the independent radio station that was the original home of Tom Scharpling's *The Best Show on WFMU*, a three-hour talk, music, and comedy show that I appeared on many times, often by phone as I walked around a noisy New York City street.

The venue held about ninety people and was sold out. Doogie Horner opened for me again. I didn't even need a ride out there, so I assume he was extra honored that I asked him to be on my show based on merit.

There were some fun audience interactions, including one with a guy who made me laugh when he said his friend didn't come to my show because he was afraid of "world-class comedy." Another guy was a tourist who'd just paid $150 to see Al Pacino do a one-man show on Broadway and planned to pay big money to see Woody Allen play clarinet with his band at the Café Carlyle. I had no choice but to point out that my show was a bargain at just $15. I repeated this several times. *Al Pacino's show was TEN times the cost of mine.* Yes, he's got better jokes, but still . . .

first performed in Nyack in the early nineties. I opened for a comic/ hypnotist, one of those guys who brings audience members onstage and gets them to do silly stuff while under his spell. He'd hypnotize the assembled group and say, "It's freezing out," and the people onstage would shiver like maniacs, while the rest of the audience laughed like maniacs. Comedy hypnotists aren't the most respected people in the comedy world, but sometimes it's fun to see something more involved than a dude speaking into a mic.

I'm pretty sure this first Nyack gig is where I had one of my memorable onstage regrets. I remember talking to a guy from the stage who worked at Burger King. I think I said, "Does your girlfriend work there, too?" He said yes. Any comic would make fun of them at that point, so I did, but I remember the guy looking a bit hurt, and I realized I'd crossed my own personal line and felt like an elitist shit. (Also, I worked at McDonald's for three weeks.)

I needed an opening act for my 2015 appearance. Joe Zimmerman couldn't do it, so he recommended a guy named Noah Gardenswartz. I wasn't familiar with Noah, so I looked him up on YouTube. He passed my "I'm impatient, so you only have ninety seconds to be funny" test, so I e-mailed him.

I fantasize about how these opening acts react when they get an e-mail from me offering them work. It probably goes something like this: *OMG! I just got an e-mail from Todd Barry! He wants me to open for him! OMG! I wonder if I'll get to talk to him!* I bet it's a lot like that.

Noah picked me up for the thirty-mile drive to Levity Live, located in the Palisades Center Mall, the eighth largest in the country. I was leaving for a solo vacation in Tokyo in two days, and I felt a cold or allergy attack coming on, so I was delighted to find that the club was located right next to a Target where I could stock up on medicine. I was more excited about finding a Target than doing the gig.

I walked into Levity Live and met the manager. I assumed they would want to drop the checks in the middle of the show, so I asked if they would suspend that tradition for my show. The manager agreed to put them down at the end but suggested Noah do an extra ten minutes of material while the audience paid. So the opening act would start the show with fifteen minutes, then I'd do an hour, and then to *bring it home*, the opening act would come *back* and do an *encore* while people were figuring out their bills? No. Noah can come up after I'm done to say good night to them, and they can pay their bill without any entertainment.

If I'm not very familiar with an opening act, I watch their entire set rather than just pacing around backstage. I want to see if we have any similar material, and it gives me a feel for what I'll be up against that night. Is the audience laughing? Are they polite? Are they smart?

At some point in his set Noah used the word "allegory" and the audience didn't shut down, so I knew it would be a good show, and it was. (Favorite moment: I sized up a guy in the audience as being nerdy, then asked him where he worked. "Game Stop," he replied. *Massive* applause.) I don't think I'd have the guts to use "allegory." I'd worry about seeing dumb, confused looks after I said it. And of course, not getting a laugh. That should be my next challenge as a comedian. A solid *allegory* joke.

DECEMBER 11, 2015—BUFFALO, NEW YORK
THE TRALF MUSIC HALL

The last time I'd played Buffalo, I'd performed at one of those music venues with a notorious bathroom. There are venues all over the world that have bathrooms so awful, they get a reputation. CBGB had that men's room stall with the door ripped off (although I understand why CBGB might not want to give some of their clientele too much *privacy*). The place in Buffalo was called Nietzsche's. The bathroom smelled terrible, but people mentioned with a chuckle, "Hey, what did you think of that bathroom, huh?" What did I think of that bathroom? Well, I feel the way you do about it, without the "thinking it's funny" part. I feel like it *smelled bad*. I don't know what you call a person who makes bathrooms smell better, but I bet there is one of them in Buffalo.

Smelly bathroom aside, the show at Nietzsche's was so great, I didn't care about the bathroom.

I returned to Buffalo in 2015 to the Tralf Music Hall. I flew on JetBlue. The flight attendant came around with their famous basket of free name-brand snacks, and I was truly bummed out when I watched a guy take two packs of cookies plus a bag of pretzels. That was for round one. I don't know why that bummed me out so much. How about starting with one pack of cookies and a bag of pretzels and see if that satiates you? I know the snacks are free, but no need to be so greedy. (FULL DISCLOSURE: I own JetBlue Airways.)

I tried to check into my hotel, but the computer at the front desk froze. If you own a hotel and your computer freezes, there's no better person to have waiting to check in than me. I will stand there until things are resolved, the whole time maintaining a warm "I get it: these things freeze sometimes" look. I can be really impatient, but the idea of berating a hotel employee who is already stressed about a computer malfunction? Not my style! Too empathetic!

I made it into the hotel, then walked around a bit. Had a nice coffee at a place called Hotel Lafayette, then a Mexican lunch at Deep South Taco. I'm not sure why I didn't get wings while I was in Buffalo. How did I not get wings? I love wings. It was probably a convenience thing. Or maybe I thought it was punk rock to not get Buffalo wings in Buffalo. *Oh, you got wings when you were in Buffalo? Let me guess, you got a cheesesteak when you were in Philly?*

One hundred nineteen people showed up to see me at the Tralf Music Hall. I joke a lot about how famous I am—but I actually am (I once got recognized two times at a *tiny* veggie burger restaurant in New York), and I wonder why I get crowds this size. One hundred nineteen is plenty of people to do a good show, but why isn't there a *frenzy* to buy tickets? I used to hire a publicist for my tours but lately had the feeling that I didn't need one. I don't think I did much press for this show. Not sure if an interview in the weekly alt paper really sells tickets, and I don't like doing press. Some of it is great, like when

I did *Fresh Air* with Terry Gross. She was prepared and is a great interviewer.

But if you do a local paper, you can hear within two questions if they even know who you are. I once did a phone interview to promote a show in Cleveland. I think it was a school paper, and the woman who called me sounded like she was twelve. She read questions that were taught to her in journalism class, including this one: "Why should people see your show instead of others in town?" What a hateful question. I answered that they should see the show that was most appealing to them. I don't promote myself like I'm a refrigerator. *Hey, Cleveland, I'll be in town January ninth. Tom Finklestern is in town that night, too, but studies show I beat him ten to one in side-by-side comedy comparisons! And my ticket price is very competitive!*

The best part of the Tralf show occurred when I talked to a woman who said she didn't like *sauces.*

"What do you mean?" I probed.

"You know when you get chicken fingers in Ohio—"

STOP. HOLD THE PHONE. WE HAVE A WINNER! How did I get lucky enough to talk to you?

"Did you say when you get chicken fingers in *Ohio?* You don't like sauces because of the chicken fingers you get in Ohio? I didn't realize Ohio was *chicken finger country!*"

She said "Yeah, you know the way they dump the sauce on the chicken fingers."

"I'm pretty sure dumping sauce on food is not just an *Ohio* thing."

It turned out she really didn't like sauces, and I guess because she is from Ohio, that's where her *sauce* aversion stems from. It would be like if I said, "I don't like when they put tomatoes on the salad, you know, like in New York."

After the show, I went to a bar with small group of people, including a friend who lives in Buffalo. I noticed a guy staring at me from another table. I figured he was at the show or just knew who I was. After a few stares he approached.

"Are you Moby?" he asked.

I laughed. "Yeah, I'm Moby. No, I'm not Moby." Most people would've stuck with the lie and enjoyed the benefits of being Moby for a night ("Can I buy you a drink, Moby?"). People love telling you about your doppelgänger. I don't know why. If someone says I look like John Malkovich or John McEnroe, all I can do is shrug. Many years ago a woman at a restaurant freaked out when she thought I was Michael Stipe from REM. Okay, she didn't really *freak out*. She got a bit excited until I told her I wasn't him. I guess it's a bit ironic I turned out to be a highly successful recording artist myself.

Final thoughts: The next morning at the breakfast buffet I heard a guy complain about finding chicken bones in front of his room (solid complaint, actually), and when I was driving to the airport I saw a billboard with this offer: three car washes and a dinner at Applebee's for $24.99. Tickets for my show were $20. No dinner. Zero car washes. Next time I'll throw in some car washes and sell that baby out!

RIDER UNIVERSITY

AUTHOR'S NOTE: First of all, let me say how thrilled I am for the chance to do an "author's note." Something about that I like. Anyway, the *note* is that I basically wrote this entire book and was ready to turn it in when I noticed that I forgot to write about this particular show. I had notes on it, but I never *wrote it up*. And now I was looking at a list of things that would trigger memories, but in most cases didn't. As a courtesy, I'm going to show you the actual list below:

Doogie, hit a car on his way out of my building.

Brought two boxes of granola bars.

Found out Justice Scalia died on the way there.

Really cold, worrying about doing a college show.

Guy named Will.

Student comic.

Show length.

Specific time or loose?
3 saxophones.
Woman who didn't like grainy food.
Air conditioning for being an RA.
Arguing over 2 restaurants in town.
Chinese food.
Crab fries.
Indira Gandhi picture.

Now I'm going to provide an *annotated* list, which includes what I remember about each item:

Doogie, hit a car on his way out of my building.

My opening act, Doogie Horner, hit a car on his way out of my building. I don't remember an altercation, so I don't even know if this counts as a *fender bender*. This was at the beginning of the trip, so I made note of it in case it turned out to be one of the highlights of the journey.

Brought two boxes of granola bars.

Oh I remember this juicy tidbit! At the beginning of the trip I told Doogie I was a bit hungry and he whipped out *two* boxes of granola bars from his bag like a hero.

Found out Justice Scalia died on the way there.

Self-explanatory.

Really cold, worrying about doing a college show.

This is a controversial *two-topic* note. It was really cold out, and I was nervous about doing a college show.

Guy named Will.

Oh Will, you must have done something interesting, but I'm afraid I forgot it.

Student comic.

Often when I do a show at a college, there are a surprising number of students who are aspiring comics, even in smaller cities. I met one of them here. If he asked for advice I probably just said, "Write lots of jokes and go on stage a lot." But I actually don't think this guy asked for my advice. Missed opportunity!

Show length.

I was worried about the minimum time I'd have to do to fulfill my obligation. This goes back to nervousness about doing college shows.

Specific time or loose?

Very similar to the previous note. I asked the dude in charge if they needed a specific show length from me, or if it could be "loose." The contract probably said I was doing an hour, so a range of forty-five minutes to one hour would be a looser interpretation of that. I mainly ask about this because no one wins if the audience hates me and I'm forced to stay on for a full hour (the only person who would win in that situation is another comic who would love watching me sweat). So if they answer "loose," then I know I'm not going to get in trouble for going short. (I should also mention that, despite my anxiety, I usually end up doing the amount of time I committed to.)

3 saxophones.

This is frustrating because I remember this being a good moment in the show, like, "Ooh, I've got something for the book," or "Ooh, I've got my *go-to* anecdote when I do the rounds of late-night TV." I'm frustrated because I don't remember the specifics, but I think a dude told me he played the saxophone, but made a point of saying he had *three* saxophones. I remember blowing people's minds when I rattled off the names of three types of saxophone. (Alto, tenor, baritone. I think those are correct.)

Woman who didn't like grainy food.

Self-explanatory, and let's face it, probably not that interesting!

Air conditioning for being an RA.

Dude in the audience was a resident assistant at his dorm. Let me know his dorm was fancier and had air conditioning.

Arguing over 2 restaurants in town.

I asked where to eat and people yelling out and shooting down each other's suggestions. I said, "Hey, let's not argue over the only two restaurants in town!"

Chinese food.

We had Chinese food backstage.

Crab fries.

I think Doogie ordered crab fries. I know I don't know if these were from the Chinese restaurant, or we got fancy and ordered backstage food from two different places like we were the Who or something.

Indira Gandhi picture.

I'm glad this is last on the list because I know exactly what this was about. There was a framed picture backstage of a woman. I knew it was someone historically important, probably because it was a school. (It would be weird if there was a big picture of the student activities director's grandmother framed in the dressing room.) We took guesses. We tried to figure out how to do a reverse Google image search. We didn't figure it out. Then at some point, someone, I think it was me, said "Indira Gandhi." I took a great picture of us.

THE LOST HORIZON

arrived for my first-ever show in Syracuse straight from the South by Southwest festival in Austin, which is always fun but also a mixed bag. The shows are usually good, the pay is bad, but you feel like you're in show business. You get a nice laminate to wear that identifies you as a comedian, and you get recognized a lot. But it's also a little intense. There are parties and mobs of people on the street, so at some point you get the "Oh God, I have to get out of here" feeling. There are no nonstop flights from Austin to Syracuse, so I had to wake up at 4:45 a.m. to make it in time for my show. I have a little trick I came up with to make early-morning flights seem less awful. I just reframe the situation. Instead of saying, "Fuck. I've got to wake up in four hours to catch a flight," I say, "I'm going to take a four-hour *nap* and then catch a flight." A four-hour nap seems extravagant in that scenario, and more than enough sleep to be refreshed. I'm pretty sure I invented the "pretend it's a nap" trick, but if you know anyone else who has suggested it, my apologies.

The flight started off fine, but then a woman announced that she was going to vomit. I think I've only been on one flight where someone puked. That's not bad considering how many times I've flown.

The pilot came on the PA and apologized for a previous announcement where he gave the wrong model of our plane. One thing I don't want to hear from a pilot is an *apology*. We all make mistakes, Captain! You got the model of the plane wrong. Big deal. As long as you know how to fly the correct model, we're all set!

I found a hippie-ish vegan café next to my hotel and ordered a delicious barbecue tempeh sandwich (no tomatoes), then took a quick walk, stopping to take a picture of a really nice credit union. And yes, I've looked at this picture many times.

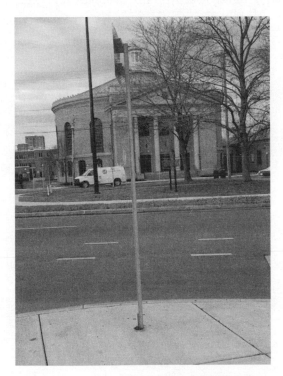

Really nice credit union. Syracuse, New York.

The venue that night was a rock club called the Lost Horizon, located next to a gentlemen's *entertainment* complex.

I did a joke about the time my ex-girlfriend and I got foot massages at a Chinese foot spa. I often start the joke by chatting with a couple in the front row, then asking, "You guys ever get massages together?" This usually gets a big laugh due to the abruptness of the question. It surprises me how few couples get massages together. This couple had never done it. The guy explained he didn't "like getting touched by another person."

"You don't like being touched by another person? What a weird thing to not like. You don't like being touched by *anyone*?"

"Well, only my wife."

There you go, buddy. I set you up nicely for that one.

THE DOCK

My first Ithaca gig was in 1999. I opened for Jon Stewart at Ithaca College. Jon had started hosting *The Daily Show* a few months prior, so he was famous, but not as huge as he is now. I was lucky enough to be one of the comics he'd used to open for him, usually at colleges. Jon's a good guy, and I always enjoy talking to him, although I remember one time when he got mad at me. We were driving somewhere listening to music, either on the radio or a mix tape. That detail isn't crucial. All I remember is a Dave Matthews Band song came on that we'd already heard earlier in the trip. I reached for the stereo to change it, and Jon snapped at me, "Hey, what are you doing? I want to hear that."

"Oh, sorry," I said as I switched it back.

I know all my super-cool fans are reading this and thinking, *The Dave Matthews Band? You should've changed it the first time that song came on! You did the right thing, Todd. Fuck Jon Stewart!*

Now now. No need for that. He wanted to hear the song again, and I was stopping him from doing that. But to be fair to me, I believe I made a reasonable assumption that since we'd heard the song already, he wouldn't want to hear it again. I wish I had his contact information; I'd like to resolve this once and for all.

The ride to Ithaca was more than four hours each way, and Jon didn't want to stay overnight, but driving back after the show seemed extreme. Also, Cornell University is in Ithaca. They have a hotel management school and a hotel run by students on-site. I think we could've gotten rooms there and been treated to hotel service by bright-eyed young people who still had a passion for hospitality. But it was Jon's show, and I was happy to work, so I dealt with it. Also, I needed a ride home.

I returned to Ithaca in 2015 years later to play a music venue called the Dock. I drove from Syracuse with Dan Shaki. The club put us up at a great upscale inn called La Tourelle. The walls of the lobby were covered with concert posters of various entertainers who have stayed there. I did not give them a poster, but maybe they would have rejected it because I'm not famous enough.

I had it in my head that I was going to eat healthy that day, so when Dan and I rolled into a neighborhood restaurant called Red's Place, I was a little shocked that I ordered "Boom Boom Shrimp" and tater tots. I don't think I was the only person who was surprised. I felt a murmur among the other patrons. *Wait, is that Todd Barry? Is he eating Boom Boom Shrimp? I believe that's a fried food item. I thought he was eating healthy today. His order of tater tots leaves me befuddled!*

Dan and I walked around the downtown area a bit. I saw a paper store with a "Be Right Back" sign on the door. For some reason, the sign made me really want to go to this paper store. Like the store was being coy. I wavered between waiting for it to open and just leaving. It was just a paper store. It's not like I was in the market for some parchment. We waited a bit longer, but they didn't return. I may never know what the inside of that paper store looks like.

About one hundred thirty people came to see me at the Dock. The backstage greenroom didn't have a bathroom, so I had to sneak out to the deck, which was right on the lake, and walk back in a different door about ten feet away. I didn't have to do that, but I wanted to.

I talked to a guy who said he doesn't like his foods mixing with each other. I'm sort of the same way, but I asked what he meant. "You know when there's a bunch of food on your plate, and the brown bean juice is going everywhere?"

"Brown bean juice? Is that what you just said? *Brown* bean juice. Not black bean juice? Not pinto bean juice? Yeah, that's a big problem, you know, when your plate is covered with *brown bean juice*." I'm not an expert on beans, but I've never heard of brown beans. They might exist. I guess I could look it up, but that wouldn't be fun. I love that this was his *go-to* example he used to illustrate his point.

I wanted to go out after the show, but it was St. Patrick's Day. The kitchen at the Dock was closed, but the cook reopened it to make me some of the best nachos I've had in years. I don't know why they were so good. I think it was the actual chip, which was lighter than what I usually get. I asked for them to be prepared "Todd Barry style." *Todd Barry–style nachos? Do you have a recipe?*

TODD BARRY–STYLE NACHOS

Chips
Cheese
Jalapeños

That's it. No shitty chunky salsa, disgusting olives, or goopy, cloying sour cream. If you have smooth salsa, that's cool. You can also shake some hot sauce on them. And maybe some brown beans if you got 'em!

THE COMEDY WORKS

W hat brings you to town?" asked the front desk clerk at the Albany Hilton Garden Inn.

"Work," I answered.

"That's boring," he fired back.

I should've responded with a "Maybe for my audiences."

Instead I took a deep breath.

Yeah, you're right. Traveling the world and telling jokes for a living is a snooze. It's so boring I had to answer your "What brings you to town?" question with "Work" to avoid the annoying conversation I'd be subjected to if I answered "I'm in town to do a comedy show" (a conversation that would occur because my job is actually fascinating).

I didn't say any of that because he was right that most people have boring jobs. I'm sure he was expecting me to answer, "You're telling *me!*"

On the way to the club, I realized I did a bad job shaving. I knew I could pull off a show with a random stubble patch, but there in the car, it was driving me crazy. We found a Dollar Tree store, the perfect place for an emergency razor run. I got a five-pack (FULL DISCLOSURE: it may have been a four-pack) of razors and walked to the cashier. A nice woman saw my sad little purchase and let me go ahead of her. I guess not many people go to the dollar store and buy one item. I was pretty happy with the razor score and yammered on to Dan about it for a good while. I mean, for a dollar, I got to relieve some anxiety and have three (or four) razors left for future shows.

Shaving in Albany, New York.

I arrived at the 144-seat club. The manager showed me the dressing room, which was downstairs, near a second showroom hosting a showcase of local comics. I whipped out the razors and used my famous *dry shave* technique to remove the indiscernible splotch of hair above my lip.

I ordered the "Boneless Wing Sampler" from a menu that also included "Fries 5 Ways." I think "boneless wings" are the same as chicken tenders. If they're not, I don't know how they're not. The food arrived and I was faced with my typical preshow dilemma: how to eat just enough so I don't feel bloated. Sometimes I'll go *off-menu* at a comedy club and say, "Can you make an extra-small order of chicken fingers for me?" If I taught a comedy course, that's the first lesson I'd give them. I'd say, "I can't teach you how to be funny, but I can tell you that it's possible to go *off-menu* at a comedy club." I didn't do that there, and the sampler was a huge helping of boneless wings with three different sauces: hot, barbecue, and the rarely-seen-on-a-comedy-club-menu sweet chili sauce (also known as "not-as-good-as-it-sounds sauce"). Next to the wings was a substantial side of fries (I don't remember which *way*).

The show was good except for one couple who were talking the whole time. I couldn't figure out their relationship. It seemed like they knew each other well, but it also seemed like a first date. The big manager who usually is in charge of throwing people out was in the back covering for a bartender who'd called in sick, so I had to deal with this awful duo for a while, saying things like "Boy, those people over there are talking quite a bit. I wonder if anyone from the club is in the room now. Boy, that would be nice in this sort of situation." They quieted down for about thirty seconds, then I did my famous "I can handle your talking, I'm just thinking of the people who paid money and got stuck sitting next to you" line. This got a cheer from the people at the next table. After a few more back-and-forths another manager got them to leave. Afterward the woman was in the lobby, looking upset in a drunken sort of way. She saw me and said, "You had me thrown out?"

"I didn't have you thrown out. The club does that."

She told me she was a big fan of mine, then asked for a picture. So here I was smiling and posing next to someone who had to be removed from my show. I think she just had too much to drink and didn't realize how loud she was; I think she was a nice person. I'm not just saying that because she also bought a poster.

I looked up "speakeasy" on Yelp and found a bar called Speakeasy 518. It had a pretty authentic vibe, with a discreet red light out front. As we were seated, the hostess informed us of their "no cell phone use" policy, as in don't pull your phones out for any reason. I've never been to a bar with this policy, and as a performer I loved it.

A friendly tattoo-covered waitress came over and took our drink orders. She had a great, confident patter, kind of like that "Hey, boys, whatcha thirsty for tonight?" That's not a direct quote. That's something I made up to convey her tone. Dan and I discussed how much of it may have been rehearsed and how much was just the way she interacted. A jazz band played in the back. During the break the bass player noticed me and told me he was a fan. He asked for a picture. I told him I felt weird about that, considering the cell phone policy. He mentioned a sketch comedy group he was in and suggested I could see a clip of them on Facebook. I deflected this offer because I don't want to be in the position of judging a total stranger's comedy. Once he recognized me it stirred up a *feeding frenzy* of recognition. The waitress walked over and sat next to me and said, "The bartender would like to get you a round of drinks."

We ordered two more drinks. I probably said, "Make it bartender's choice." Dan went the nonalcoholic route because he was driving. I'm super classy, so when the check came I knew to factor in the free drinks when figuring out the tip. But then I made a mistake, one that I shouldn't admit to. Since this book is a classic *tell-all*, I will do just that. I think the check was about $50. I factored in another $30 for the free drinks, then figured out the tip—let's say a generous 25 percent—based on that $80 total. That would be $20 that I'd add to the $50. What I did by mistake was take the $20 tip and add it to the $80 total that included the free drinks. So now I was leaving a tip on the free drinks, plus the total amount of the free drinks, so $100 for a $50 check. I realized my mistake after we left, but hey, no big deal. I'm in show business. I used to wait tables. I get it. So in my mind, I didn't overtip, I left her a "Frank Sinatra at a steak house" tip.

On the way back to New York City we stopped at a rest station. I got a spicy chicken sandwich from Roy Rogers. Guess what it came with: *Boom Boom* sauce. *Todd, didn't you have "Boom Boom Shrimp" in Ithaca? Did it freak you out that you had "Boom Boom" foods in two consecutive cities?*

It did, actually.

MARCH 25, 2016—CHARLESTON, SOUTH CAROLINA
SOTTILE THEATRE

I was originally scheduled to perform at the Charleston Comedy Festival in January. They had me in the beautiful seven-hundred-fifty-seat Sottile Theater. The festival was well promoted and the city rallied behind it, and I was on my way to selling more tickets than I've ever sold outside of New York.

Then a big snowstorm hit. I got a text from Delta Airlines saying my flight was canceled, but they rebooked me on one that arrived in Charleston at 7:52 p.m., twenty-two minutes after my show started. This flight got canceled, too, and I was rebooked on one the day after my show. At this point all I could do was try to reschedule my appearance. T. J. Miller, from the HBO show *Silicon Valley*, was supposed to do the show after mine the same night. His flight was also canceled.

The festival offered two makeup dates, March 25, which is not my birthday, and March 26, which is. I wanted to be in New York for that (not sure why—didn't really have a big party scheduled). Also if I booked the show on my birthday, I'd spend half the time onstage talking about my birthday (I'm basing this on every time I've performed on my birthday). So I picked March 25. T. J. Miller took the twenty-sixth.

I arrived at JFK on March 24 and discovered that saying, "My birthday is in two days," is not an effective way to gain entry to the Delta Sky Club lounge when you're not a member. To me it was a classic "It can't hurt to ask" scenario, and it's better than flying with regret.

I found some sort of "superfood oatmeal" at one of the airport markets. I paid for it and asked for some hot water. The woman who rang me up pointed to the hot-water dispenser, but it was empty. She then went for a walk that was longer than any other airport employee in history would have walked and returned with a cup of steaming water. When I meet an excellent employee I wish I owned a hotel or restaurant. I could slip her a card and say, "Call me if you want a new job." I wasn't hiring at Todd Barry Enterprises Ltd., but I did throw her some cash (like Sinatra at the airport).

I spotted one of those "I'm important"–type salesman guys pacing around on his cell phone. He was the ultimate "pacing businessman on a conference call" you see at the airport. (I knew full well he could be a great guy who worked as a civil rights attorney for the Southern Poverty Law Center whose only crime was making a phone call while wearing a suit, but for the sake of comedy, I need to assume the worst.)

I boarded the plane and was delighted to find I had a notable seat mate: Pacing Businessman! Any irrational hatred I had for him was defused when I watched him take a call. He talked to one guy for about thirty seconds, then said, "Hey, Bob, this plane is about to take off. I need to go. They're getting mad at me." Then he hung up. *Oh my God, he just blew that guy off!* The plane wasn't about to take off and no one was getting mad at him, especially me, because now he was my new hero.

I arrived in Charleston and was about to find some food when I heard about the death of Garry Shandling. I had done two episodes of *The Larry Sanders Show* but hadn't talked to him in years, except for a few exchanges on Twitter. I normally don't publicly comment on anyone's death—it sometimes seems like grandstanding—but this time I felt like writing something. I started a draft, then headed to a place called Leon's for lunch.

A young hostess seated me and mentioned she had seen me on the Adult Swim show *Delocated*. I ate fried chicken, looking at a draft of what I'd written about Garry, deciding whether to post it.

I got back to my hotel, logged on to my Tumblr page, and posted this:

A COUPLE OF GARRY SHANDLING MEMORIES

I was lucky enough to be on two episodes of The Larry Sanders Show. *I remember filming a take, then Garry walked over. He had a performance note for me. He didn't preface it with "This is what I want you to do." He prefaced it with "Only try this if you think it's funny." I was floored. I barely had any acting experience and couldn't believe he trusted me that much. I realized this is what made him the real deal.*

Sometime after filming the episodes I planned a trip back to LA. I think Sarah Silverman told him I was coming. Before I left there was a message on my answering machine: "Todd, it's Garry Shandling.

I heard you were coming to LA. Want to stop by the set? I think you should."

So I went to Garry's office and hung out for hours. I told him about my girlfriend at the time. After rattling off a list of her good qualities, he said, "She sounds great."

There was a pause.

"Do you want to call her?" I asked.

He smiled. "I was just about to ask."

I laughed, gave him her number, then watched Garry Shandling call my girlfriend.

I didn't regret writing it. Got some "thanks for sharing this" messages and one Facebook comment from a crazy woman who seemed to think I asked Garry to make an obscene call to my girlfriend. He just said, "Hi, Mary. This is Garry Shandling." They talked for a few minutes and he gave the phone to me. The Facebook commenter, who I don't think even realized Garry had died, mentioned that we were both probably "bad in bed."

I returned to the hotel and heard what I think was a pile driver pounding nearby. I went down to the desk to see about getting a new room. I walked up to the front desk and said, "My room is incredibly noisy. Are there any other rooms I can have?" I was ready to insist they put me in another hotel (although I've never come close to doing that).

"There's construction all over this city. There's no hotel you could go to where you wouldn't hear it," said the disarming woman at the desk, who was ready for this complaint.

Fair enough, but those rooms weren't cheap. I feel like I deserved a "Hey, before you check in, you should probably know there's going to be hours of *pile driver* noise." But she did give me some earplugs, and I downloaded a white noise app for my phone, which I haven't used since.

I found a bar called the Belmont that looked appealing, except for the two doormen out front, which always makes me uneasy. I approached them and they were friendly and attitude-free, and let me right in. I drank a glass of wine, then a *mocktail* made with *house-made* ginger beer, citrus, and pomegranate. (I asked the bartender what was in it. I'm not some *ingredient savant*.)

While I was onstage I spotted a bushy-bearded dude sitting with a woman. She was laughing, he wasn't. I've seen this before. I think it tortures some men to see another guy make their girlfriend laugh in a way they never could. After looking back at them a few times, it hit me: *Oh, the bushy-haired dude is T. J. Miller, and that must be his wife.* I was relieved. T. J. is a friend, but he's also a comedian, so I wouldn't expect him to sit there cracking up.

After the show I sent T. J. a message asking if I'd spotted him looking miserable in the audience, then met up with some local comics who were eating at the Mellow Mushroom, a pizza chain that doesn't have a New York location but seems to be everywhere else I go. At the end of the meal, the waiter asked if we wanted separate checks. There were like twelve of us. You're *encouraging* separate checks? Where I'm from they don't even install the check-splitting software in the restaurant's cash register. Before I left, the woman at the other end of the table handed me a little piece of paper. It said, *Happy Birthday! We didn't have time to buy a card.—Charleston comics.* I was really touched, although I'm pretty sure at least *one* of them had time to buy a card.

The next day at the Charleston airport I found a place that sold baked potatoes. I don't think I've ever seen this in any airport, including Boise. I'm not sure if you understand how happy this made me.

Baked potato. The Charleston airport.

A few days later I got a message from T. J. Miller. He said he wasn't even in town yet for my show and would've been laughing if he was. So it was just a different bearded dude who wasn't enjoying me.

1884 LOUNGE AT MINGLEWOOD HALL

If you told me twenty-eight years ago I'd be a successful comedian but would also get angry because my hotel didn't have a rack for hand towels, I wouldn't have believed you. Luckily for everyone around me, that was the only flaw at the Madison Hotel in Memphis. I walked into the room and was greeted by the brightest red rug I'd ever seen—much brighter than the red carpet I walked during the Venice Film Festival premiere of *The Wrestler* (you brought it up). The type of rug I would never consider buying for my own apartment but that *energized* me the second I opened the door.

I got to town the day before the show and contacted my friend Coco, whom I met on a trip to Nashville a few years earlier. She sings for a band called the Ettes and moved to Memphis with her husband, Bob Mehr, a rock journalist and biographer. I let her be my guide the next two days.

We had dinner at a place called Hog and Hominy, which Coco described as a "hipster" restaurant. Well, it was definitely a restaurant, and it was definitely good, but aside from each table having only one yellow chair, I was *by far* the only hipster thing in sight. Believe me, I looked *everywhere*. I don't necessarily *need* to eat with hipsters, but if that *is* what I'm geared up for, that is what I expect. I was livid! The restaurant's website described their food as "Italian Cooking with a Southern Drawl." I started out with a romaine salad with chicken skins (Southern) followed by a pizza (Italian), and had a glass of that Southern "sweet tea" that is so much sweeter than you ever thought possible.

After dinner we met up with Coco's husband, Bob, at the lobby bar of the Peabody hotel. It seemed like the type of classic, old-school hotel bar where they give you a tray of *high-end* bar snacks. Although I'd just eaten a whole pizza, I was excited about the prospect of *high-end* bar snacks. I'm talking about the stuff you get at the St. Regis hotel bar in New York: macadamia nuts, wasabi peas, maybe those Japanese rice crackers. I really called this one wrong, because there were no bar snacks to be found.

The next morning they were testing the fire alarms in my hotel. I've never stayed at a hotel that didn't test the fire alarms while I was there. I was given a $10 food voucher when I checked in, so I had a quick breakfast served by a waiter who was very much *in the weeds*, even though the place wasn't crowded. I was a bad waiter once myself, so I'm understanding.

After breakfast I was faced with a dilemma: Graceland or the zoo? It was my last full day in town and I decided these were my options. I don't know if zoos are the best place for animals, but when I hear "zoo" I think of animals, and I like animals. I heard the Memphis Zoo was great, but I've been to a zoo. The closest I ever came to visiting Elvis

Presley's house was on my one previous trip to Memphis in 2006, when I was on my famous "Cities I've Never Played Before" tour. I had a camera crew with me (never did anything with the footage) and we had limited time and I had limited interest, so we stopped the car and looked at Graceland for a second, then I *checked it off my list*. This time, I chose to have a fuller experience, and I was surprised by how much I liked it.

Coco picked me up and for some reason insisted on taking a detour so we could cross into Arkansas. I explained I had just been there, but she was excited by this five-minute side trip. I wanted some authentic Memphis food, so we went to Central BBQ, where Coco ordered an authentic Memphis grilled cheese sandwich off the children's menu.

We drove into the Graceland parking lot and the woman in the booth could only be described as *the nicest, kindest person I've ever met in my life*. She asked us where we were from and engaged us in a way that didn't make it look like it was just part of her job. When we pulled into the lot, all I could think is, She does that with *everyone*? A full, warm conversation with every person who parks at Graceland?

Coco had taken the Graceland tour before but joined me for my first time. I threw down over seventy dollars to rent two iPads and let John Stamos lead the way. I'm not sure how or why Mr. Stamos was chosen to narrate the iPad tour. Well, I guess I know the "how"—they offered him money and he said yes. But why did they need John Stamos for this? Because he did Elvis impressions on *Full House*? (*FULL HOUSE* FULL DISCLOSURE: I've never watched a second of *Full House*. Someone told me this after.) I felt like Elvis was the real draw here. Is there someone who's on the fence about taking the tour but decides to *pull the trigger* when they hear Stamos is involved? But John did a solid job. It was like he knew exactly where I was standing. He would say something like, "Walk around the corner, look two feet to your right, and you'll find Elvis's favorite couch," and then you would walk around the corner and find it. I was worried the tour would be overwhelming, but it wasn't. Graceland is a very big house, but I wouldn't say it is a *huge* house. After looking at the room Elvis died in and his groovy kitchen, we made our way outside, where I was faced with Elvis's grave. I forgot Elvis was buried at Graceland, so this was an unpleasant surprise. Not unpleasant like someone clipping their nails on a train, but sad. If I stare at a gravestone long enough, there's a chance I will cry. So as I stared at the graves of Elvis and his parents, I did start to well up a bit. I didn't *lose* it, but it was emotional. I have a rule: once I start crying at a museum, it's time to get coffee.

Coco took me to a place called City and State, a freestanding building that was also a store that sold clothing, home goods, and food items. A bag of cheese puffs caught my eye. The package said they were made with konjac, which I learned is some sort of Japanese yam. How much do fancy cheese puffs cost in Memphis? If I were to guess, I'd say six dollars. But I was off by eleven dollars. Yes, the cheese puffs cost seventeen dollars, and this is in Memphis. I'm sure if Elton John were in the store he'd buy a case and never eat them, but I couldn't do it. I live in New York and have never seen cheese puffs that cost seventeen dollars. I'll buy some regular cheese puffs, hunt down some konjac, and make my own.

Coco and Bob were the only people on my guest list for the show, and I did a constant scan for them while I performed. I didn't see them. I scanned several times and was getting a little angry because I hate when people are late. Halfway into my show I saw them saunter in. I was a little angry with them until I realized I had told her I went on at nine thirty when I really went on at eight thirty. A missed opportunity to be mad.

During the show I asked a guy if he had a roommate. He said he had an arrangement with his wife.

"An arrangement? What does that mean?"

"It's too complicated."

"I bet I'm smart enough to understand."

"We split the rent."

APRIL 21, 2016—MULVANE, KANSAS
KANSAS STAR CASINO

I'd told my agent I wanted to do a show in Kansas. I'd also told him I hadn't done a casino gig in a while. He knocked both of these off with one booking at the Kansas Star Casino, about a twenty-minute drive from Wichita. It would also be the fiftieth state I'd visited.

I could've stayed two nights at the casino in Mulvane, but I'd never been to Wichita and heard it was one of those up-and-coming *cool* cities, so I stayed one night at a downtown hotel so I could check it out.

A driver from the casino picked me up at the Wichita airport (which is fantastic) and drove me to the downtown Hyatt. Before dropping me off, he insisted on giving me a little tour. We drove by one area, which he warned got "unlawful after midnight." He dropped me at my hotel, and I put the "Do Not Disturb" sign on the door even though it was 6:00 p.m. and I'm pretty sure the Wichita Hyatt didn't have turn-down service.

I was contacted on Facebook by a woman named Leanne who I randomly met at a pizza place when I did a show at my alma mater, the University of Florida in Gainesville (where they welcomed me back by saying no when I asked for a lift to the show). Leanne wrote that she was living in Wichita. She had some work dinner that night, but we made plans to meet up after. I asked her for some restaurant recommendations; a place called Sabor seemed like the best choice on the list. (I found out later that it was the location of her work dinner.)

Sabor was 1.2 miles from the hotel, but I chose to walk. The woman at the front desk assured me it was safe—and it *was* before midnight—but I wasn't totally comfortable for the next twenty-five minutes or so. It's not like there were *scary* people on the street, it was more like there wasn't anybody on the street, which was more unsettling. After walking by maybe four people at the most, I arrived at Sabor. I walked in and noticed Leanne sitting with her coworkers. I said hi, and she explained it was some sort of "moms' night," where the staff takes their moms out. I've never heard of such a thing, but why not?

I sat down at a round table and looked at the menu. A familiar-looking guy walked up to my table, then *sat down* with me.

"Hey, you're Todd Barry, right?"

I said yes, without adding, "I'm also a guy eating dinner."

"I saw you walk by and thought it was you. Are you doing a show here?"

"Yes, I am."

"I saw you walk by me earlier, and I thought it might be you . . . Well, I hope you have a great trip. It was great to meet you."

When he got up and exited the restaurant, I realized, *That guy followed me in here. He wasn't even eating in the restaurant.* He looked familiar because I passed him on my walk there.

I couldn't *imagine* following someone into a restaurant and *sitting down* with them. I was once eating at the restaurant below my apartment building—a place where they knew me and would let me have a booth to myself. A woman walked over and slurred something about her boyfriend recognizing me. She then asked if she could sit down. Not ready for the question, I nodded yes. As she sat she said, "Whenever I see someone eating alone, I assume they want company."

"I actually want to be alone," I said.

She was a bit surprised but returned to her table on the other side of the restaurant. I'm not sure why I would choose the company of a drunk woman, whose boyfriend was too scared to approach me but was staring at me from across a restaurant, over being alone.

The guy in Wichita was different. I remember thinking that if you took away the "sitting down at a stranger's table uninvited" thing, it was a pleasant encounter. He was polite and didn't ask for a picture or anything.

Dipping Sauces. Wichita, Kansas.

Leanne's dinner was wrapping up and she came over to my table with a coworker. I told her what happened and she said, "Oh, that's probably just a Midwestern thing." Really? I would think a "Midwestern thing" would be to let a visiting superstar eat in peace!

Leanne, her friend, and I walked over to a wine bar a few minutes away. It was a cavernous place with some live music going on. The music was acoustic, but it was also loud, so we found a table outside. I'm not a big fan of live music outside of a concert situation. One of my favorite bars is the lobby bar at the Bowery Hotel in New York. I remember the first time I was there thinking, *Why is this place so great?* Then it hit me. *No music.* If you're a musician and offended by that, I'll add that I also wouldn't want to hang at a bar where they blasted standup comedy.

I didn't want to rush over to a casino environment the next morning, so I took an Uber to a well-reviewed coffee shop called Reverie. I sat there a bit, then witnessed the most unnecessarily polite conversation I've ever seen. It started when an employee walked over to a guy sitting near me and cleared his empty mug. "Oh, I'm sorry I didn't do that," the sitting man said.

"I was coming around to pick up mugs anyway," the barista responded. They went back and forth on this a few times, then the barista walked away. He came back and added, "Yeah, we're trying to get better about clearing the tables." I was like, *Fellas, it's okay! He was about to clear his mug, but you were walking by to clear mugs anyway. If you keep this going this can only evolve into a brawl!*

The driver from the casino picked me up at the coffee shop, then took me to the Hyatt to gather my bags so I could move. As we pulled into the casino hotel, I heard the news that Prince had died. I'd read something on Twitter earlier about a body being found at his recording studio, but it just didn't occur to me that it would be him. Prince was one of those guys I didn't listen to often, but when I did, I thought, *This guy is a genius. Why don't I listen to him more?*

My mood went from sad to angry after I checked into my hotel room. They had given me a spacious suite, which is always nice when you live in a cramped apartment. So I wheeled my luggage in, then proceeded to the bathroom. I opened the toilet, and let's just say: It needed to be flushed. Twice. I don't usually talk about toilet-related stuff, but it would be wrong to omit that from this revealing memoir. This toilet was like *bus station* awful, so I grabbed my bag—careful not to flush the *evidence*—and sprinted to the front desk.

"Yeah, I checked into my room, and the toilet wasn't flushed. It was disgusting."

"Oh, I'm sorry about that. Let's get you a new room," said the not-as-alarmed-as-she-should've-been front-desk clerk. I was happy with the new room, but I felt more of an apology was in order. Send up a basket of fruit or something.

I was given some $25 food vouchers when I checked into the hotel, so I headed into the casino. (I did a show with Louis C.K. in Atlantic City. We checked in and they gave him a $150 voucher for any restaurant in the place, and they gave me a pass to the employee cafeteria.)

A few of the restaurants weren't open for lunch, so I hit the buffet, which really is the ultimate casino experience, meaning it's something I wouldn't even consider if I weren't at a casino. It wasn't very crowded so I didn't witness much casino buffet–style gluttony. It had separate stations featuring international food. I hit the Italian station for some pasta with garlic and oil (the best way to make pasta) and a few mini slices of pizza, then I hit the salad bar. Somewhere along the way I found a sweet potato, and ended it all with a *dollop* of self-serve ice cream. I know, if there's any place where you don't have to limit yourself to a *dollop* of ice cream, it's a casino buffet. My overall memory of the show is that it wasn't bad. I'd asked my agent to book me at a casino because they can be lucrative gigs, but I never really wanted to perform at or go to a casino. I remember the first time I played Las Vegas, I ran into Steven Wright at the hotel. He told me to lower my expectations for a casino gig; the fun was going to be scaled down a bit.

I remember another casino show in Connecticut where Roberta Flack did the early show and I did the late show. Made me feel big-time that she and I were in the same room. (I watched some of her show and realized she's one of those people who've had way more hits than I remember.) The audience for my show wasn't great. Just chatty and shitty, including some awful people in the front row who got good seats because they were "high rollers." Because they regularly spent so much money at the casino, they got good seats, and the added benefit of immunity from the security staff. No one from the club was allowed to say anything to them if they disrupted the show. I'm sure if an actual fight broke out, or if someone got violent, they would have stepped in. But if it was just talking and yelling out, no problem. I returned to the same place a couple of years later and decided to ask more about this policy. "So, these high rollers up front. You can't talk to them if they yell out?" "No, I can't," said the stage manager. "So they're allowed to ruin the show?" I asked. "Yes," he answered. My goal was to get him to say out loud that they were allowing people to ruin the show, and I felt some satisfaction for achieving that goal.

A guy named Doug was in charge at the show in Kansas. I asked him how they would deal with assholes in the crowd.

"We give them one warning, then they're on their way," he said. Something about "they're on their way" reassured me and made me laugh. Doug further impressed me after I told him all my preshow needs (music and lighting preferences, dealing with jerks, selling merch, announcing the opening act). He repeated these to another staffer and remembered everything I said.

Casinos can also be a little regimented. Like, there's often a whole procedure if you want to sell merch, but Doug just let me set up a table to make some extra gambling money.

I think the show turned out good because it was more of a destination booking. I'd never done a show in Wichita, so anyone who wanted to see me in the area had to come to the casino. It wasn't like a show in Vegas, where you get people who are staying there for a few days and trying to fill their calendar with things to do, even if they won't end up enjoying them.

Highlights of the show included talking to husband-and-wife teachers, who were delighted that I didn't understand that they have schools in malls. One of them shut me down with, "You have to be from Kansas to understand." Well, I know what a school is, and I know what a mall is. Just never put them together! And I still don't know what they were talking about.

Leanne showed up with her mom and other family. I had a food voucher left. You had to cash it in all at once, so I got to be a sport who bought a round of pizzas for everyone. Not sure if I ruined it by telling them I used a voucher. I probably did.

I budgeted sixty dollars for gambling money, then my opening act Aaron Urist and I hit the $5 blackjack table. The great thing about blackjack is you can walk up to the table and say, "I don't know how to play blackjack. Will you help me?" Everyone at the table will help you. A super-cranky old man sat the end of the table. He had the "This is life or death" intensity of a man who was at a blackjack table with a minimum higher than five dollars. At some point he yelled at the dealer, "You're dealing too fast!" The dealer was replaced at some point, but I'm not sure it was due to the yelling old drunk guy. Maybe the dealer was dealing too fast, but I didn't care because I was on a winning streak. I walked out forty dollars ahead. Well, more like $35 when you factor in the $5 chip I gave to the dealer. Yes, a $5 chip for just $40 in winnings. That is truly *high roller* shit. Now give me some front-row seats to a show! I'll try to behave.

THE PYRAMID SCHEME

There's a club in Grand Rapids called Dr. Grins (I think you get it) that's on the third floor of a multilevel bar and restaurant complex called the BOB. I played there a couple of times in 2001 and 2002.

One time I had an opening act whose act was so filthy, the guy who booked the show walked over to me and apologized during the show. Luckily, right after she was done someone knocked over a whole table of drinks, so I got to *ride that wave* and have a good set. I also remember going downstairs to the restaurant and getting a salad. I told them I was the headlining comedian at the club. They told me I got a 20 percent discount on food. *Really, you can't just give me a bowl of lettuce? I just had to follow a woman who did twenty-five minutes of pussy jokes.*

I returned to Grand Rapids a few years later for something called LaughFest (I graduated from getting grins to getting actual laughs). My shows were at a music venue called the Pyramid Scheme. I walked out for the first one and saw a large video camera on a tripod set up to the left of the stage with a camera operator behind it. If I'm doing a live show, I want it to be a live show, and a camera just puts a chill on things, so I had to address it before I started, and the confused videographer shut the camera off. I hate starting a show angry. It makes me self-conscious because the audience might not understand why I'm upset.

I got booked at the Pyramid Scheme again in 2016 for the first of three not-Detroit tour dates in Michigan. I was excited about the flight because it was my first time using the new noise-canceling headphones I got for free because I tweeted at a *major noise-canceling headphone company* and asked for a "free sample." Within twenty-five minutes they asked for my address and the $300 headphones arrived a few days later. I won't tell you the brand of headphones. I want to receive free stuff and still maintain my punk cred.

I had a weird encounter as I pulled up to the hotel. I dropped my phone on the floor of the taxi. It took me a few seconds to find it, and when I did, the taxi driver thanked me several times. *You're thanking me for recovering my own phone? Thank me if I find your phone! I mean, my pleasure.*

My only plan for the day was to hit Madcap Coffee, which I'd discovered on my previous trip. I got an extravagant *late-afternoon* decaf pour-over, then thought about how I'd spend this night off. (I always wince when I order decaf, but, like eating alone, it's nothing to be embarrassed about.)

I checked to see who was playing the Pyramid Scheme that night, figuring they would let me into the show for free. It was the Reverend Horton Heat, who I'd heard was an amazing live performer, and a band called Nashville Pussy, who I'd somehow seen with David Cross when they did a *corporate gig* in New York. The third act was Lucky Tubb and the Modern Day Troubadours. On the poster it said Lucky was the "John Dillinger of honky-tonk." No argument from me.

Before I headed there I got dinner at Osteria Rossa, which was upscale but relaxed and not crowded. I felt okay sitting by myself eating some rigatoni. I even found an outlet to plug in my phone, to ensure I was like a guy I would make fun of for doing the same thing.

After dinner I walked over to the club, introduced myself, and was let in without hassle. I put my earplugs in, watched a little of Lucky Tubb and his band, then stepped out for a bit. I came back and watched Nashville Pussy for a few songs before heading to Stella's Lounge across the street. I found a seat at the end of the bar and enjoyed the Tears for Fears and B-52s mix they played. I have a history of feeling ignored by bartenders when I want to order, and I felt that as I sat there ignored for several minutes. When the bartender made it over, I ordered a cider. He put it down and said, "This is on me because I kept you waiting." First time that's happened.

I went back to the club and watched the Reverend Horton Heat. They're a *psychobilly* band, and a real pro outfit. You could sense they do a lot of gigs.

I got into ugly business mode and imagined how much each band was getting paid. I'd guess there were about three hundred people at the show, and probably about twenty musicians to pay. So some people weren't going home with much. Bands have more fun than comics (maybe?) but comics don't have to split the money.

I returned to Madcap Coffee the next day, then went looking for Bartertown Diner, a worker-owned vegetarian restaurant I discovered when I was in town for LaughFest. I remember liking the food, and I also remember asking for mustard and being told they didn't have any but offered their homemade hot sauce. I said sure, and the waitress returned with a bottle of the brightest yellow hot sauce I've ever seen. Maybe the only yellow hot sauce I've ever seen. My point is that it was 90 percent mustard.

This time I ordered a kale Caesar salad, which is to vegetarian restaurants what pad thai is to Thai restaurants. Bartertown is a *no-tipping* establishment. I don't think they had this policy the first time I went. I was uneasy about this, because I'm such a *hotshot* in the tipping department, and it feels weird to leave nothing even though they instructed you not to. They did have a great way of alleviating the guilt. On the menu they suggest you use your tip money to buy a food voucher at the register, which you pin to a bulletin aboard. Anyone can come in and grab a voucher off the board and cash it in. I doubt they ask for proof of income, so I hope the people who take advantage of this are really in need.

I never exercise on the road beyond walking around. The idea of packing sneakers seems gross—I guess I could put them in some sort of protective pouch. But this time I brought my bathing suit. Very lightweight and easy to pack, and I often forget how many hotels have indoor pools. So I put on my Speedo (boxer-short style, not "Ew, gross" style) and went downstairs. I was the only one at the pool, and there was no lifeguard. I guess hiring a full-time lifeguard at the Grand Rapids Courtyard by Marriott would seem weird, except when you think of the *saving lives* aspect of the job.

I swam three laps, and my heart was racing so hard I was frightened. I fantasized about dying alone in a Courtyard by Marriott pool. This fantasy was enough for me to call it a day, knowing that ten minutes of vigorous exercise is better than the usual no minutes.

I stopped at the lobby Starbucks for an unsweetened Passion Tango iced tea. The guy gave me a sweetened iced tea by mistake. I grabbed him by the collar and said, "What part of 'unsweetened' don't you understand?" *Whoa, Todd, seems like an overreaction. I hope you're joking.* I'm not. *Seriously, Todd, I think you are.* I might be. *Todd, you should just commit to whether or not this is a lie. Don't waver like this.* Okay. I'm not joking.

I walked over to the Pyramid Scheme and met my opening act, Brad Wenzel, a young Michigan-based comic who was recommended by the original opening act, who had to cancel.

The venue had a "no bottled water" policy, but they had a pitcher of water backstage and a tub labeled "Clean Ice." To me there's *clean* and there's *rock-club clean*, so I didn't touch it.

The crowd was enthusiastic, but there was a little pocket of dopiness. Just the occasional drunk guy who chimed in with dumb non sequiturs, prompting me to respond with, "Why would you say that?" rather than something clever. Luckily, these guys are annoying to the people around them, so it's a manageable situation.

I talked to one guy from the stage who worked for a beverage company. He lived in a three-bedroom house with his dogs and a cat for six hundred bucks a month. In these situations it's hard not to say, "You live better than me and I'm fucking famous?" So I went ahead and said something like that. Living in a bigger house trumps the obnoxiousness of saying "I'm fucking famous," so he still came out a winner.

APRIL 29, 2016—PONTIAC, MICHIGAN
THE CROFOOT BALLROOM

I couldn't find a hotel that was actually in Pontiac, Michigan, so I ended up at the Auburn Hills Hilton, one of those hotels with a huge atrium in the middle.

Normally I wouldn't eat at a chain hotel restaurant, but I was in kind of an industrial area not really conducive to strolling, so I sat down at the bar for lunch.

Two guys started chatting a few bar stools over from me. Before long the talk got pretty right-wing. I hear plenty of talk that I agree with, so this was welcome. One of them professed his support of Donald Trump, the other guy talked about the new law in North Carolina that said transgender people had to use the public restroom that matched their pre-transition gender. He added that his sister was gay but still complained about how all the liberals were hypocrites. I wanted to chime in with the classic retort "Some of them aren't," but I chose to listen. The Trump guy agreed with him on everything but kept looking over at me with each right-wing statement, almost like he was afraid of offending me or nervous that I might challenge him. It was tempting, but I don't engage in political debates at the bar of the Auburn Hills Hilton.

The hotel had a pool, so I enjoyed day two of my "swim three laps until you feel like you're going to die in a dangerous, un-lifeguarded environment" workout.

After my swim I walked to Rite Aid. I asked the cashier where to find hydrocortisone cream (for a brutal standup comedy injury I sustained), and he responded, "Erp." *Erp?* Really? I stumped you with the hydrocortisone request? Well, you better put your seat belt on, because I'm about to ask you where you keep the Advil.

I had the night off, so I met up with my improviser friend Jennifer, who drove about thirty-five minutes to pick me up so I could join her at an improv show she was attending in the Detroit suburb of Ferndale. I've never traveled that far to go to an improv show, but I was feeling a little isolated at the hotel. We arrived at the Go Comedy! Improv Theater, a place I'd performed at when I was in Detroit filming the Amy Heckerling movie *Vamps*. I improvise onstage a lot, but I don't have much experience doing actual *improv*, and I don't think I would've shined if I were in the show we were watching, *Survival Is Insufficient*, which was based on the dystopian novel *Station Eleven*. They started the show by putting this question out to the audience: "What's the least likely thing that could cause the apocalypse?" Someone answered, "Chocolate," and they were off and running.

Jen and I had the mandatory drink at a speakeasy called the Oakland, then I wanted to get an authentic "Coney" hot dog, which they do so well in Detroit, so we stopped at a place called National Coney Island. We sat at the counter of the huge restaurant and watched a male employee hurl cardboard boxes at a waitress, who didn't seem to mind. I guess when you work together awhile the rules get relaxed and you can throw shit at each other. I ordered a

Coney, which I assumed came with chili, onions, and mustard. It came out plain, so I said something to the waitress. She handed it back to the cook, who was about ten feet from me, and he said in a nonwhisper, "Oh, NOW he wants the works." Yes. I'm the *difficult guy* at the hot dog restaurant.

After the hot dog Jennifer indulged my biggest road pleasure: finding a Chase Bank ATM where I can deposit my previous night's pay.

The next day I ate a Caesar salad at the hotel. I asked for black pepper, and the waitress pointed to the salt and pepper shakers on the table. I guess she sensed that wasn't the type of *low-rent* preground black pepper I was looking for, so she said she'd check in the back for a grinder. She returned a few minutes later with a pepper grinder, then thanked me for asking for it. I'd like to think I opened up a whole new world to her and gave her an edge over the other servers.

The Crofoot Ballroom was quite impressive for a rock venue. I was told by the guy in charge that it's less filthy than most rock clubs because they also use it for weddings. No need to be too clean if it's just people at a concert. There was a spacious greenroom. The promoter gave us some menus from nearby restaurants so we could order dinner. I wanted to order Thai food, but Brad said he'd never tried it. I guess we could've ordered from separate restaurants, but that seemed excessive. I wanted to be gracious, but not as much as I wanted Thai food. I asked Brad if he wanted recommendations.

"What would you order if you were, say, feeding it to a child or dog?" he asked.

Chicken satay and a side of steamed rice it is!

The audience was pretty dead for the opening acts, then a bit reserved for me, but I think it may have had something to do with the high ceilings (ah yes, the *high ceilings* excuse).

The show started off weird because someone's phone went off. I soon realized it was mine. I felt like an evangelist who was busted soliciting a prostitute. *You don't really practice what you preach!* There was another distraction: the TVs were on when I walked onstage. I mentioned something and a guy walked around with some sort of extension rod designed to turned them off. I've done shows in sports bars during "the big game" and they don't turn them off. I enjoyed this exchange with a dude in the crowd:

"What kind of rent do you pay?" I asked.

"Apartment rent."

"I wasn't asking what *style* of rent you paid."

When I checked out I overheard a woman at the front desk complaining about something; I couldn't hear the specifics. The front desk offered her seven thousand Hilton HHonors reward points. She wasn't having that, so the offer went up to ten thousand. All I could think of was that hotel I stayed at in Kansas where I was greeted with a full, unflushed toilet upon arrival. That was part of the Hilton family. Wasn't offered one reward point. What are the chances that this woman's grievance was worse than mine? *Very* unlikely. I might still try to get those points.

The next day I grabbed lunch at P. F. Chang's, which I'd been deprived of on my trip to Arlington. The night started great when I asked, "How are you?" to the waiter and he answered, "Too blessed to be stressed." But the real highlight was at the end of the meal when I opened my fortune cookie and read this: *Your humor will come in handy in your next job.* I posted a picture of the fortune on Instagram and Twitter. My brother happens to know a *bigwig* at P. F. Chang's. He sent him the post, and the guy sent me a $100 gift card!

THE LOFT

I thought I'd been to Lansing, Michigan, before, but I was actually in East Lansing, which I'm told is a completely different city. So this was my Lansing debut.

We arrived at the Loft for a sound check and I was a little scared. Not scared, just not encouraged. It was just so obviously a rock club, with a high stage with a barricade similar to the one at the club in Honolulu.

They'd set up round tables up front, which gave it a "cabaret meets a place where half the audience pukes during the show" vibe. I didn't love the round tables and was debating whether to have them removed and just leave the chairs. Then I thought of a brilliant idea.

"Can you add a row or two of chairs in front of these round tables?

"I can do that," said the man in charge.

He added the chairs and fixed the whole problem.

I was proud of myself for thinking of this solution. Better to have the audience right up front as opposed to scattered at round tables.

Fixing the seating felt good, but for some reason I was worried the crowd might be rowdy. There were too many sections to the room. Too much potential for them to lose focus.

The show started with a local emcee. He did a good job but was having problems with the mic. It's a precarious thing to replace a mic once the show has started. But it's a comedy show and not a play, so everything can seem like part of the show. I consulted with the sound guy about how to remedy this. We could have sent a note onstage that said, "A new mic is coming," but that would've been a lot of work, and he was about to introduce Brad, so it was possible we didn't have time. The only solution left was for the sound guy to bring out a new mic to applause that was meant for Brad.

It turns out my premonition about the crowd's being rowdy was off. It was the best of the Michigan shows.

Brad and I sold merch with a great view of a woman passed out in the sea of now-empty chairs. It was hard to know what made her pass out. I wouldn't wish an alcohol problem on her, so I'd like to think I bored her into that state.

I had my posters to sell, and Brad had brought Frisbees that said, "Brad Wenzel Sold Me This Frisbee." He hadn't brought them to Grand Rapids and had forgotten to plug them in Pontiac, so tonight he had some catching up to do.

I'm sure most people were in the merch line for my poster, but because I'm a great guy, I did a little suggestive selling, which I learned at a festival in New York with bands like Sonic Youth and Iggy and the Stooges. I had three different CDs out to sell, and one of the pro merch guys—who I think worked for Iggy Pop—agreed to sell them for me. I watched a kid approach the table and look at my trio of equally amazing CDs. The merch guy said, "You want all three?" The kid looked up and said, "Uh, yeah." I doubt that would've happened if the guy didn't put it in his head.

My posters were priced at $15. Brad's Frisbees were $5. Almost everyone who approached had a twenty-dollar bill, so I'd point to Brad's Frisbee and say, "You want the *party pack* for twenty dollars?" Most people chose the party pack (perhaps because, like me, they wanted to be associated with the word "party") and Brad went home with some extra cash to supplement the shit pay he got for opening for me.

Brad's girlfriend, Emily, had graduated from college that day and he'd brought her straight from the ceremony to the show. We all went on a search for late-night food. We found a place called the Fleetwood Diner. It didn't just look open, it looked like the world's most open diner. Lights on, people sitting at tables eating. But Brad's girlfriend walked in ahead of us and got a stern "It's takeout only" from the woman at the counter.

We moved on to Corey's Lounge, which, according to Yelp, seemed like a cool neighborhood bar and restaurant. We walked in and immediately felt like we'd crashed a private party. I got the feeling everyone knew each other, almost like it was a meet-up of swingers. There was a band set up and no hostess greeted us. We walked into one of the dining rooms and it didn't feel like a lot of food was being served. I'm sure it wasn't a meet-up of swingers, and if I had it to do over again I would've said, "Let's do this," instead of, "Let's get out of here," just for the full experience.

Emily knew about a late-night pizza chain called Pizza House in East Lansing. We pulled up, and unlike the diner, this place seemed closed when it was open. Perfect way to end the tour. Nice thin-crust pizza. Menu that listed "oregano" as a topping. I didn't throw down $1.95 for that, but they're right. It is a topping.

CONCLUSION

I believe it was Jane Austen who said, "Always end your first book abruptly, with something about a pizza topping." So I did. (But it really was crucial that I made at least sixteen references to pizza before I said good-bye.)

This is my first book, so I'm not sure how people are experiencing it. Is it a beach book? Are people reading it in order or bouncing around? Like maybe skipping the Asheville chapter because they know someone they don't like who went to college there.

The only thing I'm sure of is my book will be a colossal hit with book clubs. I can see people sitting around, drinking wine, and debating over their favorite "Todd didn't like his hotel room" story. Inevitably someone will ask, "Why do you think Todd limited this book to shows that were in secondary markets?"

"That question is meaty enough to keep us here another three hours," someone will add.

At this point I'll kick the front door down and walk into the living room. After the gasps subsided I'll say, "That was a great question!" I'll pour myself a generous glass of Pinot Grigio, then grab a seat on the couch. "Why did I limit it to secondary markets?"

"Was that always the intention of the book?" an eager young grad student named Malcolm will ask.

"To be fully candid, Malcolm, I didn't realize this was the point of the book when I was writing it."

"You didn't? What did you think the point was?" he'll interject.

"Well, Malcolm, if you'd give me a fucking second to finish a thought . . . ," I'll say, briefly losing my cool. "Many times I asked myself, 'Why *am* I writing this book about touring secondary markets? What an excruciatingly boring topic. Aren't books supposed to have a theme? Is there an *overarching* theme to this? A *through-line*? I mean, all these experiences could've happened in big cities.'"

"I have to say I had that same thought," a tattooed poet named Joan will add.

"Well, Joan, you're right. All these things could've happened in big cities, and I realized *that* is the point: doing a show in Lansing, Michigan, is not much different than doing a show in Detroit. You come into town, find some coffee, some local food. You get a nice little group of people showing up. You tell some jokes, then you leave."

"So you're saying people are pretty much the same anywhere, and we shouldn't have preconceptions about someone's intellect or capacity to understand humor based on their city of residence?" an essayist named Evan will say.

"Couldn't have said it better myself, Evan!" I'll say while placing a piece of brie on a cracker.

"Well, now that that's settled, what happens now?" Evan will ask.

"I guess it's time for a book signing. Line forms behind Joan!"

ACKNOWLEDGMENTS

So I was all ready to slap together my "thank you(s)"—I'm sorry, I mean *acknowledgments*—for this book. I figured I'd think of all the people who helped my career and a few assorted friends and family, write up a little list, and then I'd be done. No one is going to read that part, anyway. Out of curiosity, I checked the acknowledgments section in my friend Dave Hill's book, *Dave Hill Doesn't Live Here Anymore*. Well, it turns out a list wasn't good enough for old Dave. He wrote *paragraphs* of names, with explanations as to why each person should be acknowledged (except for me, who only got his name listed), along with little quips and jokes. Like it wasn't enough work to write a whole book—now I have to write *paragraphs* of gratitude. Nope. I was too lazy to write a dedication.

So thanks to these people (and one cat):

My family
My editors Natasha Simons and Jeremie Ruby-Strauss
Richard Abate
Dave Becky
Josh Lieberman
Everyone at 3 Arts Entertainment
Joseph Schwartz

Mike Berkowitz

Everyone at APA

Theresa Dooley

Everyone at Gallery Books

Sheila Kenny

Dave Hill

Gregg Turkington

Sarah Silverman

Louis C.K.

Tom Ryan

Doug Stanhope

Marc Maron

Jen Kirkman

Jesse Eisenberg

Judd Apatow

Tim Heidecker

Jim Gaffigan

"Weird Al" Yankovic

All the venue owners and bookers who let me perform in their cities

Dan Shaki, Doogie Horner, Sean Keane, Joe Zimmerman, Andrew Polk, Noah Gardenswartz, and all the comedians I worked with on the tour

Marlene

Sunflower